"InterVarsity Press is do~~ing~~ ~~~ _The Contemporary Christian_ back into print—~~slightly~~, helpfully rearranged, and broken into short, reader-friendly books. The result is a boon to a new generation of readers who will greatly benefit, as many have before, from Stott's thorough grounding in Scripture, unusual help for living the Christian life, and perceptive interaction with the contemporary world."

Mark Noll, author of _The Rise of Evangelicalism_

"I have long benefited from the work of John Stott because of the way he combines rigorous engagement of the biblical text and careful engagement with the culture of his day. The God's Word for Today series presents Stott at his very best. This series displays his commitment to biblical authority, his zeal for the mission of the church, and his call to faithful witness in the world. Stott's reflections here are a must-read for church leaders today."

Trevin Wax, director of Bibles and reference at LifeWay Christian Resources, author of _This Is Our Time_ and _Eschatological Discipleship_

"Imagine being a child overwhelmed by hundreds of jigsaw puzzle pieces—you just can't put them together! And then imagine a kindly old uncle comes along and helps you put the whole thing together piece by piece. That is what it felt like reading John Stott's _The Contemporary Christian_. For those of us who feel we can't get our head around our Bible, let alone our world, he comes along and, with his staggering gifts of clarity and insight, helps us step by step to work out what it means to understand our world through biblical lenses. It's then a great blessing to have Tim Chester's questions at the end of each chapter, which help us think through and internalize each step."

Rico Tice, senior minister for evangelism, All Souls Langham Place, London, coauthor of _Christianity Explored_

"Vintage Stott, with all that that implies. In it, as usual, we find him digesting and deploying a wide range of material with a symmetry matching that of Mozart, a didactic force like that of J. C. Ryle, and a down-to-earth common sense that reminds us of G. K. Chesterton. It is really a pastoral essay, a sermon on paper aimed at changing people . . . an outstandingly good book."
J. I. Packer, in *Christianity Today*

"In my formative years as a young Christian, I was acutely aware of the fact that I faced many challenges to Christian thinking and behavior. Few writers helped me understand how I should respond to these challenges and think and live as a Christian as much as John Stott did. The challenges of faithfulness to God's way are more acute and complex today than when I was a young Christian. In these little books you find the essence of Stott's thinking about the Christian life, and it is refreshing to read again and see how relevant and health giving this material is for today. I'm grateful to InterVarsity Press and to Tim Chester for making Stott's thinking accessible to a new generation."
Ajith Fernando, teaching director, Youth for Christ, Sri Lanka

"It is always refreshing, enlightening, and challenging reading from the pen of John Stott. I am totally delighted that one of his most significant works will continue to be available, hopefully for more decades to come. The way Stott strives to be faithful to the Word of God and relevant to his world—secularized Western society—as the locus for the drama of God's action is exemplary, especially for those of us ordained to the service of the church in our diverse contexts. I highly commend the God's Word for Today series to all who share the same pursuit—listening intently to God's Word and God's world, hearing and obeying God."
David Zac Niringiye, author of *The Church: God's Pilgrim People*

"I am delighted that a new generation will now be able to benefit from this rich teaching, which so helped me when it first appeared. As always with John Stott, there is a wonderful blend of faithful exposition of the Bible, rigorous engagement with the world, and challenging applications for our lives."

Vaughan Roberts, author of *God's Big Picture*

"Technology has enabled more voices to clamor for our attention than ever before; while at the same time, people's ability to listen carefully seems to have deteriorated like never before. John Stott's speaking and writing was renowned for two things in particular. He taught us how to listen attentively to God in order to live faithfully for God, and he too modeled how to listen to the world sensitively in order to communicate God's purposes intelligibly. He taught us to listen. That is why it is such a thrill to see *The Contemporary Christian* carefully revived in a new format as this series for a new generation of readers. As we read, may we listen well!"

Mark Meynell, director (Europe and Caribbean) of Langham Preaching, Langham Partnership, author of *When Darkness Seems My Closest Friend*

All the royalties from this book have been irrevocably assigned to Langham Literature. Langham Literature is a ministry of Langham Partnership, founded by John Stott. Chris Wright is the International Ministries Director.

Langham Literature provides Majority World preachers, scholars and seminary libraries with evangelical books and electronic resources through publishing and distribution, grants and discounts. They also foster the creation of indigenous evangelical books in many languages through writers' grants, strengthening local evangelical publishing houses and investment in major regional literature projects.

For further information on Langham Literature, and the rest of Langham Partnership, visit the website at www.langham.org.

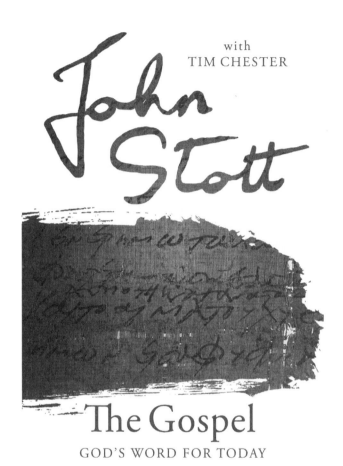

with
TIM CHESTER

John
Stott

The Gospel

GOD'S WORD FOR TODAY

An imprint of InterVarsity Press
Downers Grove, Illinois

InterVarsity Press, USA
P.O. Box 1400
Downers Grove, IL 60515-1426, USA
ivpress.com
email@ivpress.com

Inter-Varsity Press, England
36 Causton Street
London SW1P 4ST, England
ivpbooks.com
ivp@ivpbooks.com

This volume has been adapted from John Stott, The Contemporary Christian (1992), and is one of five titles published in this format in the God's Word for Today series, with extra text, including questions, by Tim Chester. Published by Inter-Varsity Press, England, as The Contemporary Christian series.

InterVarsity Press®, USA, is the book-publishing division of InterVarsity Christian Fellowship/USA® and a member movement of the International Fellowship of Evangelical Students. Website: intervarsity.org.

Inter-Varsity Press, England, originated within the Inter-Varsity Fellowship, now the Universities and Colleges Christian Fellowship, a student movement connecting Christian Unions in universities and colleges throughout Great Britain, and a member movement of the International Fellowship of Evangelical Students. Website: uccf.org.uk.

Cover design: Mark Read
Image: © The University of Manchester

USA ISBN 978-0-8308-4366-4 (print)
USA ISBN 978-0-8308-6446-1 (digital)
UK ISBN 978-1-78359-928-8 (print)
UK ISBN 978-1-78359-929-5 (digital)

Typeset in Great Britain by CRB Associates, Potterhanworth, Lincolnshire
Printed in the United States of America ♾

Library of Congress Cataloging-in-Publication Data
A catalog record for this book is available from the Library of Congress.

P	22	21	20	19	18	17	16	15	14	13	12	11	10	9	8	7	6	5	4	3	2	1
Y	39	38	37	36	35	34	33	32	31	30	29	28	27	26	25	24	23	22	21	20	19

Contents

About the authors   viii

Preface   ix

A note to the reader   xi

Series introduction: the Contemporary Christian –
    the then and the now   1

The Gospel: introduction   9

  1 The human paradox   11

  2 Authentic freedom   24

  3 Christ and his cross   35

  4 The relevance of the resurrection   48

  5 Jesus Christ is Lord   63

Conclusion: the now and the not yet   77

Notes   87

About the authors

John Stott had a worldwide ministry as a church leader, a Bible expositor and the author of many award-winning books. He was Rector Emeritus of All Souls, Langham Place, London, and Founder-President of the Langham Partnership.

Tim Chester is Pastor of Grace Church, Boroughbridge, North Yorkshire, Chair of Keswick Ministries and the author of more than forty books.

Preface

To be 'contemporary' is to live in the present, and to move with the times without worrying too much about the past or the future.

To be a 'contemporary Christian', however, is to live in a present that is enriched by our knowledge of the past and by our expectation of the future. Our Christian faith demands this. Why? Because the God we trust and worship is 'the Alpha and the Omega . . . who is, and who was, and who is to come, the Almighty',[1] while the Jesus Christ we follow is 'the same yesterday and today and for ever'.[2]

So this book and series are about how Christians handle time – how we can bring the past, the present and the future together in our thinking and living. Two main challenges face us. The first is the tension between the 'then' (past) and the 'now' (present), and the second the tension between the 'now' (present) and the 'not yet' (future).

The Introduction opens up the first problem. Is it possible for us truly to honour the past and live in the present at the same time? Can we preserve Christianity's historic identity intact without cutting ourselves off from those around us? Can we communicate the gospel in ways that are exciting and modern without distorting or even destroying it? Can we be authentic and fresh at the same time, or do we have to choose?

The Conclusion opens up the second problem: the tension between the 'now' and the 'not yet'. How far can we explore and experience everything that God has said and done through Christ without straying into what has not yet been revealed or given? How can we develop a proper sense of humility about a future yet to unfold without becoming complacent about where we are in the present?

In between these enquiries into the influences of the past and the future comes an exploration about our Christian responsibilities in the present.

Preface

This series is about questions of doctrine and discipleship under the five headings: 'The Gospel' (the book you are holding in your hands), 'The Disciple', 'The Bible', 'The Church' and 'The World', though I make no attempt to be systematic, let alone exhaustive.

In addition to the topic of time, and the relations between past, present and future, there is a second theme running through this series: the need for us to talk less and listen more.

I believe we are called to the difficult and even painful task of 'double listening'. We are to listen carefully (although, of course, with differing degrees of respect) both to the ancient Word and to the modern world, in order to relate the one to the other with a combination of faithfulness and sensitivity.

Each book in this series is an attempt at double listening. It is my firm conviction that if we can only develop our capacity for double listening, we will avoid the opposite pitfalls of unfaithfulness and irrelevance, and truly be able to speak God's Word to God's world with effectiveness today.

Adapted from the original Preface by John Stott in 1991

A note to the reader

The original book entitled *The Contemporary Christian*, on which this volume and series are based, may not seem 'contemporary' to readers more than a quarter of a century later. But both the publisher and John Stott's Literary Executors are convinced that the issues which John Stott addresses in this book are every bit as relevant today as when they were first written.

The question was how to make this seminal work accessible for new generations of readers. We have sought to do this in the following ways:

- The original work has been divided into a series of several smaller volumes based on the five major sections of the original.
- Words that may not resonate with the twenty-first-century reader have been updated, while great care has been taken to maintain the thought process and style of the author in the original.
- Each chapter is now followed by questions from a current best-selling Christian author to aid reflection and response.

Lovers of the original work have expressed delight that this book is being made available in a way that extends its reach and influence well into a new century. We pray that your life will be enriched as you read, as the lives of many have already been greatly enriched by the original edition.

Series introduction
The Contemporary Christian –
the then and the now

The expression 'the contemporary Christian' strikes many as a contradiction in terms. Isn't Christianity an antique relic from the remote past, irrelevant to people in today's world?

My purpose in this series is to show that there is such a thing as 'contemporary Christianity' – not something newfangled, but original, historic, orthodox, biblical Christianity, sensitively related to the modern world.

Christianity: both historical and contemporary

We begin by reaffirming that Christianity is a historical religion. Of course, every religion arose in a particular historical context. Christianity, however, makes an especially strong claim to be historical because it rests not only on a historical *person*, Jesus of Nazareth, but on certain historical *events* which involved him, especially his birth, death and resurrection. There is a common thread here with the Judaism from which Christianity sprang. The Old Testament presents God not only as 'the God of Abraham, Isaac and Jacob', but also as the God of the covenant that he made with Abraham, and then renewed with Isaac and Jacob. Again, he is not only 'the God of Moses', but is also seen as the Redeemer responsible for the exodus, who went on to renew the covenant yet again at Mount Sinai.

Christians are forever tethered in heart and mind to these decisive, historical events of the past. We are constantly encouraged in the

Bible to look back to them with thankfulness. Indeed, God deliberately made provision for his people to recall his saving actions on a regular basis. Supremely, the Lord's Supper or Holy Communion enables us to call the atoning death of Christ regularly to mind, and so bring the past into the present.

But the problem is that Christianity's foundational events took place such a long time ago. I had a conversation with two brothers some years ago – students who told me they had turned away from the faith of their parents. One was now an agnostic, the other an atheist. I asked why. Did they no longer believe in the truth of Christianity? No, their dilemma was not whether Christianity was *true*, but whether it was *relevant*. How could it be? Christianity, they went on, was a primitive, Palestinian religion from long ago. So what on earth did it have to offer them, living in the exciting, modern world?

This view of Christianity is widespread. The world has changed dramatically since Jesus' day, and goes on changing with ever more bewildering speed. People reject the gospel, not necessarily because they think it false, but because it no longer resonates with them.

In response to this we need to be clear about the basic Christian conviction that God continues to speak through what he has spoken. His Word is not a prehistoric fossil, but a living message for the contemporary world. Even granted the historical particularities of the Bible and the immense complexities of the modern world, there is still a fundamental correspondence between them. God's Word remains a lamp to our feet and a light for our path.[1]

At the same time, our dilemma remains. Can Christianity both retain its authentic identity *and* demonstrate its relevance?

The desire to present Jesus in a way that appeals to our own generation is obviously right. This was the preoccupation of the German pastor Dietrich Bonhoeffer while in prison during World War 2: 'What is bothering me incessantly,' he wrote, 'is the question . . . who Christ really is for us today?'[2] It is a difficult question. In answering it, the church has tended in every generation to develop images of Christ which deviate from the portrait painted by the New Testament authors.

Attempting to modernize Jesus

Here are some of the church's many attempts to present a contemporary picture of Christ, some of which have been more successful than others in remaining loyal to the original.

I think first of *Jesus the ascetic* who inspired generations of monks and hermits. He was much like John the Baptist, for he too dressed in a camel's hair cloak, wore sandals or went barefoot, and munched locusts with evident relish. But it would be hard to reconcile this portrait with his contemporaries' criticism that he was a party-goer who 'came eating and drinking'.[3]

Then there was *Jesus the pale Galilean*. The apostate emperor Julian tried to reinstate Rome's pagan gods after Constantine had replaced them with the worship of Christ, and is reported as having said on his deathbed in AD 363, 'You have conquered, O Galilean.' His words were popularized by the nineteenth-century poet Swinburne:

Thou hast conquered, O pale Galilean;
The world has grown grey from thy breath.

This image of Jesus was perpetuated in medieval art and stained glass, with a heavenly halo and a colourless complexion, eyes lifted to the sky and feet never quite touching the ground.

In contrast to the presentations of Jesus as weak, suffering and defeated, there was *Jesus the cosmic Christ*, much loved by the Byzantine church leaders. They depicted him as the King of kings and Lord of lords, the creator and ruler of the universe. Yet, exalted high above all things, glorified and reigning, he seemed aloof from the real world, and even from his own humanity, as revealed in the incarnation and the cross.

At the opposite end of the theological spectrum, the seventeenth- and eighteenth-century deists of the Enlightenment constructed in their own image *Jesus the teacher of common sense*,[4] entirely human and not divine at all. The most dramatic example is the work of Thomas Jefferson, President of the United States from 1801 to 1809. Rejecting the supernatural as incompatible with reason, he produced his own edition of the Gospels, in which all miracles and mysteries were systematically eliminated. What is left is a guide to a merely human moral teacher.

In the twentieth century we were presented with a wide range of options. Two of the best known owe their popularity to musicals. There is *Jesus the clown* of *Godspell*, who spends his time singing and dancing, and thus captures something of the gaiety of Jesus, but hardly takes his mission seriously. Somewhat similar is *Jesus Christ Superstar*, the disillusioned celebrity who once thought he knew who he was, but in Gethsemane was no longer sure.

The late President of Cuba, Fidel Castro, frequently referred to Jesus as 'a great revolutionary', and there have been many attempts to portray him as *Jesus the freedom fighter*, the urban guerrilla, the first-century Che Guevara, with black beard and flashing eyes, whose most characteristic gesture was to overthrow the tables of the moneychangers and to drive them out of the temple with a whip.

These different portraits illustrate the recurring tendency to update Christ in line with current fashions. It began in the apostolic age, with Paul needing to warn of false teachers who were preaching 'a Jesus other than the Jesus we [apostles] preached'.[5] Each succeeding generation tends to read back into him its own ideas and hopes, and create him in its own image.

Their motive is right (to paint a contemporary portrait of Jesus), but the result is always distorted (as the portrait is unauthentic). The challenge before us is to present Jesus to our generation in ways that are both accurate and appealing.

Calling for double listening

The main reason for every betrayal of the authentic Jesus is that we pay too much attention to contemporary trends and too little to God's Word. The thirst for relevance becomes so demanding that we feel we have to give in to it, whatever the cost. We become slaves to the latest fad, prepared to sacrifice truth on the altar of modernity. The quest for relevance degenerates into a lust for popularity. For the opposite extreme to irrelevance is accommodation, a feeble-minded, unprincipled surrender to the spirit of the time.

God's people live in a world which can be actively hostile. We are constantly exposed to the pressure to conform.

Thank God, however, that there have always been those who have stood firm, sometimes alone, and refused to compromise. I think of Jeremiah in the sixth century BC, and Paul in his day ('everyone . . . has deserted me'),[6] Athanasius in the fourth century and Luther in the sixteenth.

In our own day we too need to resolve to present the biblical gospel in such a way as to speak to modern dilemmas, fears and frustrations, but with equal determination not to compromise it in so doing. Some stumbling-blocks are intrinsic to the original gospel and cannot be eliminated or soft-pedalled in order to make it easier to accept. The gospel contains some features so alien to modern thought that it will always appear foolish, however hard we strive to show that it is 'true and reasonable'.[7] The cross will always be an assault on human self-righteousness and a challenge to human self-indulgence. Its 'scandal' (stumbling-block) simply cannot be removed. The church speaks most authentically not when it has become indistinguishable from the world around us, but when its distinctive light shines most brightly.

However keen we are to communicate God's Word to others, we must be faithful to that Word and, if necessary, be prepared to suffer for it. God's word to Ezekiel encourages us: 'Do not be afraid of them . . . You must speak my words to them, whether they listen or fail to listen, for they are rebellious.'[8] Our calling is to be faithful and relevant, not merely trendy.

How, then, can we develop a Christian mind which is both shaped by the truths of historic, biblical Christianity and also fully immersed in the realities of the contemporary world? We have to begin with a double refusal. We refuse to become either so absorbed in the Word that we *escape* into it and fail to let it confront the world, or so absorbed in the world that we *conform* to it and fail to subject it to the judgment of the Word.

In place of this double refusal, we are called to double listening. We need to listen to the Word of God with expectancy and humility, ready for God perhaps to confront us with a word that may be disturbing and uninvited. And we must also listen to the world around us. The voices we hear may take the form of shrill and strident protest. There will also be the anguished cries of those who are suffering, and the pain, doubt, anger, alienation and even despair of those who are at odds with God. We listen to the Word with humble reverence, anxious to understand it, and resolved to believe and obey what we come to understand. We listen to the world with critical alertness, anxious to understand it too, and resolved not necessarily to believe and obey it, but to sympathize with it and to seek grace to discover how the gospel relates to it.

Everybody finds listening difficult. But are Christians sometimes less good at listening than others? We can learn from the so-called 'comforters' in the Old Testament book of Job. They began well. When they heard about Job's troubles, they came to visit him and, seeing how great his sufferings were, said nothing to him for a whole week. If only they had continued as they began, and kept their mouths shut! Instead, they trotted out their conventional view – that every sinner suffers for his own sins – in the most insensitive way. They did not really listen to what Job had to say. They merely repeated their own thoughtless and heartless claptrap, until in the end God stepped in and rebuked them for having misrepresented him.

We need to cultivate 'double listening', the ability to listen to two voices at the same time – the voice of God through the Bible and the voices of men and women around us. These voices will often contradict one another, but our purpose in listening to them both is to discover how they relate to each other. Double listening is indispensable to Christian discipleship and to Christian mission.

It is only through this discipline of double listening that it is possible to become a 'contemporary Christian'. We bring 'historical' and 'contemporary' together as we learn to apply the Word to the world, proclaiming good news that is both true and new.

To put it in a nutshell, we live in the 'now' in the light of the 'then'.

The Gospel
Introduction

Christianity is not a religion, let alone one religion among many. It is God's good news for the world. The Christian gospel has both a divine origin (it comes from God) and a human relevance (it speaks to our condition). So, before we ask the question, 'What is the gospel?', we must explore the logically prior question, 'What is a human being?'

Chapter 1 ('The human paradox') is an attempt to do justice to what the Bible teaches and our own experience endorses. We will see both the glory and the shame of our humanness, both our dignity as creatures made in God's image and our depravity as sinners under his judgment. Chapter 2 then presents what is traditionally called 'salvation' in terms of 'Authentic freedom'.

Chapters 3 and 4 handle the central themes of the death and resurrection of Jesus which secured our freedom. I begin by tackling the five main objections to the gospel of Christ crucified and then the denials of his bodily resurrection. Then I argue that the significance of the resurrection of Jesus set out in the New Testament depends on the traditional belief that it involved the raising and transforming of his body.

In chapter 5, we look at the far-reaching implications, for both faith and life, of the seemingly innocent affirmation that Jesus Christ is Lord. Taking Christ's lordship seriously leads to radical discipleship.

1

The human paradox

What does it mean to be human?

Twice this question is posed in the Old Testament – in Psalm 8:3–4 and Job 7:17. And on both occasions the writer expresses surprise, even incredulity, that God should pay so much attention to his human beings. For we are insignificant in comparison to the vastness of the universe, and impure in contrast to the brightness of the stars.

There are at least three major reasons why this question is important.

Personally speaking, to ask 'What is humanity?' is another way of asking 'Who am I?' There is no more important field for search or research than our own personal identity. Until we have found ourselves, we can't grow into personal maturity, nor fully discover anything else. 'Who am I?' and 'Do I have any significance?' are universal cries.

Professionally, whatever our work may be, we are inevitably involved in serving people. Doctors and nurses have patients, teachers pupils, lawyers and social workers clients, members of parliament constituents, and business people customers. How we treat others in our work depends almost entirely on how we view them.

Politically, the nature of human beings is central to any political theory. Do human beings have an absolute value because of which they must be respected? Or is their value only relative to the state because of which they may be exploited? More simply, are institutions servants of the people, or are the people servants of institutions? As John S. Whale has written, 'ideologies . . . are really anthropologies'; they are different doctrines of humanity.[1] Answers to the question 'What is humanity?' tend to be either too naive in their optimism, or too negative in their pessimism, about the human condition.

Secular humanists are generally optimistic. Although they believe that *Homo sapiens* is nothing but the product of a random evolutionary process, they nevertheless believe that human beings are continuing to evolve, have limitless potential, and will one day take control of their own development. But such optimists do not take seriously enough the moral failings of humanity and our self-centredness, which have constantly undermined progress and led to disillusionment in social reformers.

Existentialists, on the other hand, tend to be extremely pessimistic. Because there is no God, they say, there are no values, ideals or standards any more. And, although we need somehow to find the courage to be, our existence has neither meaning nor purpose. Everything is ultimately absurd. But such pessimists overlook the love, joy, beauty, truth, hope, heroism and self-sacrifice which have enriched the human story.

What we need, therefore, to quote J. S. Whale again, is 'neither the easy optimism of the humanist, nor the dark pessimism of the cynic, but the radical realism of the Bible'.[2]

Our human dignity

The Bible affirms the intrinsic value of human beings from the first chapter onwards.

> Then God said, 'Let us make mankind in our image, in our likeness, so that they may rule over the fish in the sea and the birds in the sky, over the livestock and all the wild animals, and over all the creatures that move along the ground.'
> So God created mankind in his own image.

in the image of God he created them;
male and female he created them.

God blessed them and said to them, 'Be fruitful and increase in number; fill the earth and subdue it. Rule over the fish in the sea and the birds in the sky and over every living creature that moves on the ground.'[3]

There has been a long-standing debate about the meaning of the divine 'image' or 'likeness' in human beings, and what it is that distinguishes us from other animals. Keith Thomas collected a number of suggestions in his book *Man and the Natural World*.[4] He points out that a human being was described by Aristotle as a political animal, by Thomas Willis as a laughing animal, by Benjamin Franklin as a tool-making animal, by Edmund Burke as a religious animal, and by James Boswell, the gourmet, as a cooking animal.[5] Other writers have focused on some physical feature of the human body. Plato made much of our erect posture, so that animals look down, and only human beings look up to heaven. Aristotle added the peculiarity that only human beings are unable to wiggle their ears.[6] A seventeenth-century doctor was greatly impressed by our intestines, by their 'anfractuous circumlocutions, windings and turnings', whereas in the late eighteenth century Uvedale Price drew attention to our nose: 'Man is, I believe, the only animal that has a marked projection in the middle of the face.'[7]

Scholars who are familiar with ancient Egypt and Assyria, however, emphasize that in those cultures the king or emperor was regarded as the 'image' of God, representing him on earth, and that kings had images of themselves erected in their provinces to symbolize the extent of their authority. Against that background God the Creator entrusted a kind of royal (or at least vice-regal) responsibility to all human beings, appointing them to 'rule' over the earth and its creatures, and 'crowning' them with 'glory and honour' to do so.[8]

In the unfolding narrative of Genesis 1 it is clear that the divine image or likeness is what distinguishes humans (the climax of creation) from animals (whose creation is recorded earlier). A continuity between humans and animals is implied. For example, they share 'the breath of life'[9] and the responsibility to reproduce.[10] But there is also a radical discontinuity between them, in that only human beings are said to be 'like God'. This emphasis on the unique distinction between humans and animals keeps recurring throughout Scripture. The argument takes two forms. We should be ashamed both when human beings behave like animals, descending to their level, and when animals behave like human beings, doing better by instinct than we do by choice. As an example of the former, people are not to be 'senseless and ignorant' and behave like 'a brute beast', or 'like the horse or the mule, which have no understanding'.[11] As an example of the latter, we are rebuked that oxen and donkeys are better at recognizing their master than we are,[12] that migratory birds are better at returning home after going away,[13] and that ants are more industrious and make better provision for the future.[14]

Returning to the early chapters of Genesis, all God's dealings with Adam and Eve presuppose their uniqueness among his creatures. He addresses them in a way that assumes they can understand. He tells them which fruit they may eat and not eat, taking for granted an ability to discern between a permission and a prohibition, and choose between them. He planted the garden, and then put Adam in it 'to work it and take care of it',[15] thus initiating a conscious, responsible partnership between them in cultivating the soil. He created them male and female, pronounced solitude 'not good', instituted marriage for the fulfilment of their love, and blessed their union. He also 'walked in the garden in the cool of the day', desiring their companionship, and missed them when they hid from him.[16] It is not surprising, therefore, that this cluster of five privileges (understanding, moral choice, creativity, love and fellowship with God) are all regularly mentioned in Scripture, and continue to be recognized in the contemporary world as constituting the unique distinction of our 'humanness'.

To begin with, there is *our self-conscious rationality*. It is not only that we as humans are able to think and to reason. There is a lot of talk today of 'artificial intelligence'. And it is true that computers can process vast quantities of data much faster than we can. They have a form of memory (they can store information) and a form of speech (they can communicate their findings). But there is still one thing (thank God!) they cannot do. They cannot originate new thoughts; they can only 'think' what is fed into them. Human beings, however, are original thinkers. More than that. We can do what we (author and reader) are doing at this very moment: we can stand outside ourselves, look at ourselves, and evaluate ourselves, asking ourselves who and what we are. We are self-conscious and can be self-critical. We are also restlessly inquisitive about the universe. True, as one scientist said to another, 'Astronomically speaking, man is infinitesimally small.' 'That is so,' responded his colleague, 'but then, astronomically speaking, man is the astronomer.'

Next, there is *our ability to make moral choices*. Human beings are moral beings. It is true that our conscience reflects our upbringing and culture, and is therefore fallible. Nevertheless, it remains on guard within us, like a sentinel, warning us that there is a difference between right and wrong. It is also more than an inner voice. It represents a moral order outside and above us, to which we sense an obligation. We have a strong urge to do what we perceive to be right, and feelings of guilt when we do what we believe to be wrong. Our whole moral vocabulary (commands and prohibitions, values and choices, obligations, conscience, freedom and will, right and wrong, guilt and shame) is meaningless to animals. True, we can train our dog to know what it is allowed and forbidden. And when it disobeys, and cringes from us by a reflex action, we can describe it as looking 'guilty'. But it has no sense of guilt; it knows only that it is going to be punished.

Third, there are *our powers of artistic creativity*. God not only calls us into a responsible stewardship of the natural environment, and into partnership with himself in subduing and developing it for the common good, but he has also given us innovative skills through science and art to do so. We are 'creative creatures'. That is, as creatures we depend upon our Creator. But having been created in our Creator's likeness, he has given us the desire and the ability to be creators too. So we draw and we paint, we build and we sculpt, we dream and we dance, we write poetry and we make music. We are able to appreciate what is beautiful to the eye, the ear and the touch.

In the next place, there is *our capacity for relationships of love*. God said, 'Let us make man in our image . . . So God created man in his own image . . . male and female he created them.' Although we must be careful not to deduce from this text more than it actually says, it is surely legitimate to say that the plurality within the Creator ('Let *us* make man') was expressed in the plurality of his creatures ('male and female he created them'). It became even clearer when Jesus prayed for his own people 'that all of them may be one, Father, just as you are in me and I am in you'.[17] And this unity of love is unique to human beings. Of course, all animals mate, many form strong pairings, most care for their young, and some are gregarious. But the love which binds human beings together is more than an instinct, more than a disturbance in the endocrine glands. It has inspired the greatest art, the noblest heroism, the finest devotion. God himself is love, and our experiences of loving are an essential reflection of our likeness to him.

Fifth, there is *our insatiable thirst for God*. All human beings are aware of an ultimate personal reality, whom we seek, and in relation to whom alone we know we will find our human fulfilment. Even when we are running away from God, instinctively we know that we have no other resting place, no other home. Without him we are lost, like waifs and strays. Our greatest claim to nobility is our created capacity to know God, to be in personal relationship with him, to love him and to worship him. Indeed, we are most truly human when we are on our knees before our Creator.

It is in these things, then, that our distinctive humanness lies, in our God-given capacities to think, to choose, to create, to love and to worship. 'In the animal,' by contrast, wrote Emil Brunner, 'we do not see even the smallest beginning of a tendency to seek truth for truth's sake, to shape beauty for the sake of beauty, to promote righteousness for the sake of righteousness, to reverence the Holy for the sake of its holiness ... The animal knows nothing "above" its immediate sphere of existence, nothing by which it measures or tests its existence ... The difference between man and beast amounts to a whole dimension of existence.'[18]

No wonder Shakespeare made Hamlet break out into his eulogy: 'What a piece of work is a Man! how noble in reason! how infinite in faculty! in action how like an angel! in apprehension how like a god! the beauty of the world! the paragon of animals!'[19]

I wish I could stop there and we could live the rest of our lives glowing with unadulterated self-esteem! But sadly there is another, darker side to our humanity, of which we are all too well aware, and to which Jesus himself drew our attention.

Our human depravity

Jesus once said,

Listen to me, everyone, and understand this. Nothing outside a person can defile them by going into them. Rather, it is what comes out of a person that defiles them ... For it is from within, out of a person's heart, that evil thoughts come – sexual immorality, theft, murder, adultery, greed, malice, deceit, lewdness, envy, slander, arrogance and folly. All these evils come from inside and defile a person.[20]

Jesus did not teach the fundamental goodness of human nature. He undoubtedly believed the Old Testament truth that humankind, male and female, were made in the image of God, but he also believed that this image had been marred. He taught the worth of human beings, not least by devoting himself to their service, but he also taught our unworthiness. He did not deny that we can give 'good things' to others, but he also added that while doing good, we do not escape the designation 'evil'.[21] And in these verses he made important assertions about the extent, nature, origin and effect of evil in human beings.

First, he taught *the universal extent of human evil*. He was not portraying the criminal segment of society or some particularly degraded individual or group. On the contrary, he was in conversation with refined, righteous and religious Pharisees. Indeed, it is often the most upright people who are the most keenly aware of their own degradation. Take, for example, Dag Hammarskjöld, Secretary-General of the United Nations from 1953 to 1961, a deeply committed public servant whom W. H. Auden described as 'a great, good and lovable man'. Yet his view of himself was very different. In his collection of autobiographical pieces entitled *Markings*, he wrote of 'that dark counter-centre of evil in our nature', so that we even make our service of others 'the foundation for our own life-preserving self-esteem'.[22]

Second, Jesus taught *the self-centred nature of human evil*. In Mark 7 he listed thirteen examples. What is common to them all is that each is an assertion of the self either against our neighbour (murder, adultery, theft, false witness and covetousness – breaches of the second half of the Ten Commandments – are all included) or against God ('pride and folly' being defined in the Old Testament as denials of God's sovereignty and even of his existence). Jesus summarized the Ten Commandments in terms of love for God and neighbour, and every sin is a form of selfish revolt against God's authority or our neighbour's welfare.

Third, Jesus taught *the inward origin of human evil*. Its source is not found in a bad environment or a faulty education (although both can have a powerful conditioning influence on impressionable young people). Instead, its source must be traced to our 'heart', our inherited and twisted nature. One might almost say that Jesus introduced us to Freudianism before Freud. At least what he called the 'heart' is roughly equivalent to what Freud called the 'unconscious'. It resembles a very deep well. The thick deposit of mud at the bottom is usually unseen, and even unsuspected. But when the waters of the well are stirred by the winds of violent emotion, the most evil-looking, evil-smelling filth bubbles up from the depths and breaks the surface – rage, hate, lust, cruelty, jealousy and revenge. In our most sensitive moments we are appalled by our potential for evil. Superficial remedies just will not do.

Fourth, Jesus spoke of *the defiling effect of human evil*. 'All these evils come from inside,' he said, 'and defile a person.'[23] The Pharisees considered defilement to be largely external and ceremonial. They were preoccupied with clean foods, clean hands and clean vessels. But Jesus insisted that defilement is internal and moral. What renders us unclean in God's sight is not the food which goes into us (into our stomach), but the evil which comes out of us (out of our heart).

All those who have caught even a momentary glimpse of the holiness of God have been unable to bear the sight, so shocked have they been by their own contrasting uncleanness. Moses hid his face, afraid to look at God. Isaiah cried out in horror at his own pollution and lostness. Ezekiel was dazzled, almost blinded, by the sight of God's glory, and fell face down on the ground.[24] As for us, even if we have never glimpsed the splendour of Almighty God like these men, we know we are unfit to enter his presence in time or in eternity.

In saying this, we have not forgotten our human dignity. Yet we must do justice to Jesus' own evaluation of evil in our human condition:

- It is universal (in every human being without exception).
- It is self-centred (a revolt against God and neighbour).
- It is inward (issuing from our heart, our fallen nature).
- It is defiling (making us unclean and therefore unfit for God).

We who were made by God like God are disqualified from living with God.

The resulting paradox

Here, then, is the paradox of our humanness: our dignity and our depravity. We are capable both of the loftiest nobility and of the basest cruelty. One moment we can behave like God, in whose image we were made, and the next like the beasts, from whom we were meant to be completely distinct. Human beings are the inventors of hospitals for the care of the sick, universities for the acquisition of wisdom, parliaments for the just rule of the people, and churches for the worship of God. But they are also the inventors of torture chambers, concentration camps and nuclear arsenals. Strange, bewildering paradox! Noble and ignoble, rational and irrational, moral and immoral, God-like and bestial! As C. S. Lewis put it through Aslan, 'You come of the Lord Adam and the Lady Eve. And that is both honour enough to erect the head of the poorest beggar, and shame enough to bow the shoulders of the greatest emperor on earth.'[25]

I do not know any more eloquent description of the human paradox than one that was given by Richard Holloway:

I am dust and ashes, frail and wayward . . . riddled with fears, beset with needs . . . the quintessence of dust and unto dust I shall return . . . *But* there is something else in me . . . Dust I may be, but troubled dust, dust that dreams, dust that has strange premonitions of transfiguration, of a glory in store, a

destiny prepared, an inheritance that will one day be my own
... I am a riddle to myself, an exasperating enigma ... this
strange duality of dust and glory.[26]

Faced with the horror of their own dichotomy, some people are
foolish enough to imagine that they can sort themselves out,
banishing the evil and liberating the good within them. The classic
expression both of our human ambivalence and of our hopes of self-
salvation was given by Robert Louis Stevenson in his famous tale *The
Strange Case of Dr Jekyll and Mr Hyde* (1886). Henry Jekyll was a
wealthy and respectable doctor, inclined to religion and philanthropy.
But he was conscious that his personality had another, darker side,
so that he was 'committed to a profound duplicity of life'. He
discovered that 'man is not truly one, but truly two'. He began to
dream of solving the problem of his duality by ensuring both sides
of his character were 'housed in separate identities', the unjust going
one way, and the just the other. So he developed a drug by which he
could assume the deformed body and evil personality of Mr Hyde,
his alter ego, through whom he gave vent to his passions – hatred,
violence, blasphemy and even murder.

At first Dr Jekyll was in control of his transformations, and
boasted that the moment he chose, he could be rid of Mr Hyde for
ever. But gradually Hyde gained ascendancy over Jekyll, until he
began to become Hyde involuntarily, and only by great effort could
resume his existence as Jekyll. 'I was slowly losing hold of my
original and better self, and becoming slowly incorporated with my
second and worse.' Finally, a few moments before his exposure and
arrest, he committed suicide. The truth is that every Jekyll has
their Hyde, whom they cannot control and who threatens to take
them over.

This continuing paradox of our humanness throws much light
on both our private and our public lives. I will give an example of
each.

I begin with *personal redemption*. Because evil is so deeply entrenched within us, we are utterly unable to save ourselves. So our most urgent need is redemption. We need a new beginning in life that offers us both a cleansing from the pollution of sin and a new heart, even a new creation, with new perspectives, new ambitions and new powers. And, because we were made in God's image, such redemption is possible. No human being is irredeemable. For God came after us in Jesus Christ, and pursued us even to the desolate agony of the cross. There he took our place, bore our sin and died our death in order that we might be forgiven. Then he rose, ascended and sent the Holy Spirit, who is able to enter our personality and change us from within. If there is any better news for the human race than this, I for one have never heard it.

My second example of our paradoxical human situation relates to *social progress*. The fact that people – even very degraded people – retain vestiges of the divine image in which they were created is evident. This is why, on the whole, all human beings prefer justice to injustice, freedom to oppression, love to hatred, and peace to violence. This everyday observation raises our hopes for social change. Most people cherish visions of a better world. The complementary fact, however, is that human beings are 'twisted with self-centredness' (as a former Archbishop of Canterbury, Michael Ramsey, used to define original sin), and this places limits on our expectations. The followers of Jesus are realists, not Utopians. It is possible to improve society, but the perfect society, 'the home of righteousness',[27] awaits the return of Jesus Christ.

Reflection questions from Tim Chester

1 Do you tend to be optimistic or pessimistic about other people?
2 What have you seen today that reflects the dignity of human beings? What have you seen today that reflects the depravity of human beings?

3 John Stott lists five characteristics of human dignity: our self-conscious rationality, our ability to make moral choices, our powers of artistic creativity, our capacity for relationships of love and our insatiable thirst for God. For each of these five characteristics, identify one thing you could do that would enable you to be more fully human.

4 How should our similarities with, and differences from, animals shape the way we treat them?

5 How should the paradox of human dignity and human depravity affect our approach to politics? What happens if we ignore human dignity? What happens if we ignore human depravity?

6 What does the paradox of human dignity and human depravity suggest is humanity's greatest need?

2

Authentic freedom

One of the best ways of sharing the gospel today is to present it in terms of freedom. At least three arguments may be used.

First, freedom is an extremely appealing topic. There is a widespread distrust of authority, tradition and institutions in our culture, seen as synonymous with a worldwide quest for freedom. Many people are obsessed with it, and are spending their lives in pursuit of it. For some it is *national* freedom, emancipation from external rule. For others it is *civil* rights, as they protest against ethnic, sexual or gender discrimination. Yet others are preoccupied with the search for *economic* freedom, freedom from hunger, poverty and unemployment. At the same time, all of us are concerned for our *personal* freedom. Even those who campaign most vigorously for the other freedoms I have mentioned (national, civil and economic) often know that they are not liberated people themselves. They cannot always put a name to the tyrannies that oppress them. Yet they feel frustrated, unfulfilled and unfree.

John Fowles, the writer of *The French Lieutenant's Woman* which was made into a film starring Meryl Streep and Jeremy Irons, was once asked in an interview, 'Is there a particular picture of the world that you would like to develop in your writing? Something that has remained important to you?' 'Freedom, yes,' John Fowles replied, 'how you achieve freedom. That obsesses me. All my books are about that.'[1]

Second, 'freedom' is a great Christian word. Jesus Christ is portrayed in the New Testament as the world's supreme liberator. 'The Spirit of the Lord is on me,' he claimed, applying an Old Testament prophecy to himself, 'because he has anointed me to preach good news to the poor. He has sent me to proclaim freedom for the prisoners and recovery of sight for the blind, to set the oppressed free, to proclaim the year of the Lord's favour.'[2] Whether Jesus intended the poor, the prisoners, the blind and the oppressed to be understood as material or spiritual categories or both (the question continues to be hotly debated), the good news he proclaimed to them was certainly 'freedom' or 'release'. Later in his public ministry he added the promise: 'If the Son sets you free, you will be free indeed.'[3] Then the apostle Paul became the champion of Christian liberty and wrote, 'It is for freedom that Christ has set us free. Stand firm, then, and do not let yourselves be burdened again by a yoke of slavery.'[4] For those who find 'salvation' a bit of meaningless religious jargon, and even an embarrassment, 'freedom' is an excellent substitute. To be saved by Jesus Christ is to be set free.

Third, freedom is much misunderstood. Even those who talk loudest and longest about freedom have not always paused first to define what they are talking about. A notable example is the Marxist orator who was waxing eloquent on the street corner about the freedom we would all enjoy after the revolution. 'When we get freedom,' he cried, 'you'll all be able to smoke cigars like that', pointing at an opulent gentleman walking by.

'I prefer my cigarette,' shouted a heckler.

'When we get freedom,' the Marxist continued, ignoring the interruption and warming to his theme, 'you'll all be able to drive in cars like that', pointing to a sumptuous Mercedes that was driving by.

'I prefer my bike,' shouted the heckler.

And so the dialogue continued, until the Marxist could bear his tormentor no longer. Turning on him, he said, 'When we get freedom, you'll do what you're told.'

The negative: freedom *from*

So what is freedom? A true definition is bound to begin negatively. We have to identify the forces that tyrannize us and so inhibit our freedom. Only then can we grasp how Christ is able to liberate us.

First, Jesus Christ offers us *freedom from guilt*. We should be thankful for the reaction against Freud's insistence that feelings of guilt are pathological, symptoms of mental sickness. Some doubtless are, especially in certain kinds of depression, but not all guilt is false guilt. On the contrary, an increasing number of contemporary psychologists and psychotherapists, even if they are not Christians, are telling us that we must take our responsibilities seriously. The late Dr Hobart Mowrer of the University of Illinois, for example, understood human life in contractual terms and saw 'sin' as a breach of contract for which restitution must be made. Certainly, the Bible has always emphasized both our obligations as human beings and our failure to meet them. In particular, we have asserted ourselves against the love and authority of God, and against the welfare of our neighbours. To use straight-forward Christian language, we are not only sinners, but guilty sinners, and our conscience confirms this. According to one of Mark Twain's witticisms, 'Man is the only animal that blushes – or needs to.'[5]

No-one is free who is unforgiven. If I were not sure of God's mercy and forgiveness, I could not look you in the face, or (more importantly) God. I would want to run away and hide, as Adam and Eve did in the Garden of Eden. The 'cover-up' did not start with contemporary politicians, but in Eden. I would certainly not be free. Not long before she died, in a moment of surprising candour on television, Marghanita Laski, well-known secular humanist and novelist, said, 'What I envy most about you Christians is your forgiveness; I have nobody to forgive me.'

'But,' as Christians want to shout from the housetops, echoing the psalmist, 'there is forgiveness with God.'[6] For in his love for sinners like us, God entered our world in the person of his Son. Having lived a life of perfect righteousness, he identified himself in his death with our unrighteousness. He bore our sin, our guilt, our death in our place, in order that we might be forgiven.

So freedom begins with forgiveness. I remember a university student who had been brought up in spiritism who was taken to a Christian meeting where he heard the gospel. The following weekend the battle for his soul began in earnest, until (as he wrote later) he cried in despair to Jesus Christ to save him. Then, he said, 'he really came to me. I felt actual, real love. I can't describe it. It was just pure beauty and serenity. And despite the fact that I knew nothing about salvation and sin, and did not even know what they meant, I just *knew* I was forgiven . . . I was unbelievably happy.'

Second, Jesus Christ offers us *freedom from ourselves*. Talking once with some Jewish believers, he said, 'If you hold to my teaching, you are really my disciples. Then you will know the truth, and the truth will set you free.' They were indignant. How dare he say that they needed to be liberated? 'We are Abraham's descendants,' they cried, 'and have never been slaves of anyone. How can you say that we shall be set free?'

Jesus replied, 'Very truly I tell you, everyone who sins is a slave to sin.'[7]

So, if guilt is the first slavery from which we need to be freed, sin is the second. What does that mean? Like 'salvation', 'sin' is a word that belongs to the traditional vocabulary of Christians. 'I am not a sinner,' people often say, because they seem to associate sin with specific and rather sensational misdeeds like murder, adultery and theft. But 'sin' has a much wider connotation than that. I can remember what a revelation it was to me to learn that what the Bible means by 'sin' is primarily self-centredness. For God's two great commandments are first, that we love him with all our being, and second, that we love our neighbour as we love ourselves. Sin, then, is the reversal of this order. It is to put ourselves first, proclaiming our own autonomy. We put our neighbour next when it suits our convenience, and God somewhere in the background.

The fact that self-centredness is common to all human experience is clear from the rich variety of words in our language which are compounded with 'self'. There are more than fifty that have a pejorative meaning – words like self-applause, self-absorption, self-assertion, self-advertisement, self-indulgence, self-gratification, self-glorification, self-pity, self-importance, self-interest and self-will.

Our self-centredness is a terrible tyranny. Malcolm Muggeridge used to speak of 'the dark little dungeon of my own ego'. And what a dark dungeon it is! To be engrossed in our own selfish concerns and ambitions, without regard either for the glory of God or for the good of others, is to be confined in the most cramped and unhealthy of prisons.

Yet Jesus Christ, who rose from the dead and is alive, can liberate us. It is possible for us to know 'the power of his resurrection'.[8] Or, to put the same truth in different words, the living Jesus can enter our personality by his Spirit and turn us inside out. Not of course that Christians claim to be perfect, but by the power of his indwelling Spirit we have at least begun to experience a transformation from self to un-self. Our previously closed personality is starting to unfold to Christ, like a flower opening to the warmth of the sun.

Third, Jesus Christ offers us *freedom from fear*. The ancient world into which he came lived in dread of the powers which, it was believed, inhabited the stars. Still today, adherents of traditional religion are haunted by malevolent spirits that need to be placated. Lives of modern people are also overshadowed by fear. There are the common fears that have always plagued human beings – the fear of sickness, bereavement, old age and death, together with the fear of the unknown, the occult and environmental disaster. Most of us have also sometimes suffered from irrational fears. It is extraordinary how many educated people entertain superstitious fears. They touch wood, cross their fingers, carry charms and avoid the number thirteen, believing it to be unlucky. Many high-rise hotels in the United States have no thirteenth floor. As you go up in the elevator, the numbers jump from 12 to 14. People are too super-stitious to sleep on the thirteenth floor, without realizing that it is still the thirteenth even if you call it the fourteenth! In Britain there are more adults who read their horoscope each week than read their Bible.

All fear brings a measure of paralysis. Nobody who is afraid is free. Moreover, fear is like fungus: it grows most rapidly in the dark. It is essential, therefore, to bring our fears out into the light and look at them, especially in the light of the victory and supremacy of Jesus Christ. For he who died and rose has also been exalted to his Father's right hand, and everything has been put 'under his feet'.[9] So where are the things of which we were previously afraid? They are under the feet of the triumphant Christ. It is when we see them there that their power to terrify is broken.

That fear and freedom are mutually incompatible was illustrated for me once by a young African lecturer. We had been discussing the need for Christians to take a greater interest in natural history as God's creation. 'Before I became a Christian,' he responded, 'I was afraid of many things, especially snakes. But now I find it hard to kill one because I enjoy watching them. I thank God that now I am really free.'

The positive: freedom *for*

So far we have connected the tyrannies that impede our freedom to the three major events in the experience of Jesus Christ: his death, resurrection and exaltation. There is freedom from guilt because he died for us, freedom from self because we may live in the power of his resurrection, and freedom from fear because he reigns, with all things under his feet.

It is a serious error, however, to define freedom in entirely negative terms, even if dictionaries make this mistake. According to one, freedom is 'the absence of hindrance, restraint, confinement, repression', while according to another, to be free is to be 'not enslaved, not imprisoned, unrestricted, unrestrained, unhampered'. Every negative, however, has its positive counterpart. The true cry for freedom is not only for rescue from some tyranny, but also for liberty to live a full and meaningful life. Once a country has been delivered from a dictatorship, it is free to develop a new national identity. Once the press is delivered from governmental control and censorship, it is free to publish the truth. Once a minority is delivered from discrimination, it is free to enjoy self-respect and dignity. For it is nationhood which is denied when a country is not free, truth when the press is not free and self-respect when a minority is not free.

What, then, is the positive freedom of human beings? Michael Ramsey, a former Archbishop of Canterbury, once preached a series of four sermons, which were published under the title *Freedom, Faith and the Future*. In the first he posed the question: 'We know what we want to free men *from*. Do we know what we want to free men *for*?' He went on to answer his own question. Our striving for those freedoms 'which most palpably stir our feelings' (e.g. freedom from persecution, arbitrary imprisonment, crippling hunger and poverty) should always be 'in the context of the more radical and revolutionary issue of the freeing of man from self and for the glory of God'.[10]

It is this question of what we are set free for by Christ that we need to pursue. The principle is this: *true freedom is freedom to be our true selves, as God made us and meant us to be.* How can this principle be applied?

We must begin with God himself. Have you ever considered that God is the only being who enjoys perfect freedom? You could argue that he is not free. For his freedom is certainly not absolute in the sense that he can do absolutely anything. Scripture itself tells us that he cannot lie, tempt or be tempted, or tolerate evil.[11] Nevertheless, God's freedom is perfect in the sense that he is free to do absolutely anything that he wills to do. God's freedom is freedom to be always entirely himself. There is nothing arbitrary, moody, capricious or unpredictable about him. He is constant, steadfast, unchanging. In fact, the main thing Scripture says he 'cannot' do (cannot because he will not) is contradict himself. 'He cannot deny himself.'[12] To do this would not be freedom, but self-destruction. God finds his freedom in being himself, his true self.

What is true of God the Creator is also true of all created things and beings. Absolute freedom, freedom unlimited, is an illusion. If it is impossible for God (which it is), it is most certainly impossible for God's creation. God's freedom is freedom to be himself; our freedom is freedom to be ourselves. The freedom of every creature is limited by the nature which God has given it.

Take fish. God created fish to live and thrive in water. Their gills are adapted to absorb oxygen from water. Water is the only element in which a fish can find its 'fishiness', its identity as a fish, its fulfilment, its freedom. True, it is limited to water, but in that limitation is liberty. Supposing you keep a tropical fish at home. It lives not in a modern, rectangular, aerated tank, but in one of those old-fashioned, Victorian, spherical goldfish bowls. And supposing your fish swims round and round its bowl until it finds its frustration unbearable. So it decides to make a bid for freedom and leaps out of its confinement. If somehow it manages to leap into a pond in your garden, it will increase its freedom. It is still in water, but there is more water to swim in. If instead it lands on the carpet, then its attempt to escape spells not freedom, but death.

What, then, about human beings? If fish were made for water, what are human beings made for? I think we have to answer that if water is the element in which fish find their fishiness, then the element in which humans find their humanness is love, the relationships of love. Morris West gives a striking example of this in his book *Children of the Sun*, which tells the story of the *scugnizzi*, the abandoned street children of Naples, and of Father Mario Borelli's love for them. 'There is one thing about us (that is Neapolitans),'

Mario said to Morris, 'that never changes. *We have need of love as a fish has need of water*, as a bird has need of air.'[13] He went on to explain that every single one of the *scugnizzi* he knew 'had left home because there was no longer any love for him'.

But it is not just the world's street children who need to love and to be loved, and who discover that life spells love. It is all of us. It is in love that we find and fulfil ourselves. The reason for this is not hard to find. It is that God is love in his essential being, so that when he made us in his own image, he gave us a capacity to love as he loves. It is not a random thing, therefore, that God's two great commandments are to love him and each other, for this is our destiny. A truly human existence is impossible without love. Living is loving, and without love we wither and die. As Robert Southwell, the sixteenth-century Roman Catholic poet, expressed it: 'Not when I breathe, but when I love, I live.' He was probably echoing Augustine's remark that the soul lives where it loves, not where it exists.

True love, however, places constraints on the lover, for love is essentially self-giving. And this brings us to a startling Christian paradox. True freedom is freedom to be my true self, as God made me and meant me to be. And God made me for loving. But loving is giving, self-giving. Therefore, in order to be myself, I have to deny myself and give myself. In order to be free, I have to serve. In order to live, I have to die to my own self-centredness. In order to find myself, I have to lose myself in loving.

True freedom is, then, the exact opposite of what many people think. It is not being free from responsibility to God and others so I can live for myself. That is bondage to my own self-centredness. Instead, true freedom is freedom from my silly little self so I can live responsibly in love for God and others.

Yet the secular mind cannot come to terms with this Christian paradox of freedom through love. For example, Françoise Sagan, the French novelist, once told an interviewer she was perfectly satisfied with her life and had no regrets.

'You have had the freedom you wanted?'

'Yes.' Then she qualified her statement. 'I was obviously less free when I was in love with someone . . . But one's not in love all the time. Apart from that . . . I'm free.'[14]

The implication was clear: love inhibits liberty. The more you love, the less free you are, and vice versa. Presumably, therefore, the way to be completely free is to avoid all the entanglements of love, indeed to give up loving altogether.

But Jesus taught the opposite in one of his favourite sayings, one that he seems to have quoted in different forms and contexts. He said, 'For whoever wants to save their life will lose it, but whoever loses their life for me and for the gospel will save it.'[15] I used to imagine that Jesus was referring to martyrs who lay down their life for him. And the principle he is enunciating certainly includes them. But the 'life' he is talking about, which can be either saved or lost, is not our physical existence (*zōē*), but our soul or self (*psychē*). It is a word that is often used instead of the reflexive 'himself' or 'herself'. One could, then, perhaps paraphrase Jesus' words like this: 'If you insist on holding on to yourself, and on living for yourself, and refuse to let yourself go, you will lose yourself. But if you are willing to give yourself away in love, then, at the moment of complete abandonment, when you imagine that everything is lost, the miracle takes place and you find yourself and your freedom.' It is only sacrificial service, the giving of the self in love to God and others, which is perfect freedom.

Authentic freedom, then, combines the negative (freedom from) with the positive (freedom for). Or, to put it another way, it brings together freedom from tyranny and freedom under authority. Jesus illustrated this in one of his best-known invitations:

Come to me, all you who are weary and burdened, and I will give you rest. Take my yoke upon you and learn from me, for I am gentle and humble in heart, and you will find rest for your souls. For my yoke is easy and my burden is light.[16]

There are actually two invitations here with a single promise. The promise is 'rest', which seems to include the notion of freedom. 'I will give you rest,' says Jesus. 'You will find rest for your souls.' But to whom does he promise rest? He gives it first to those who come to him 'weary and burdened', for he lifts their burdens and sets them free. Second, he gives it to those who take his yoke upon them and learn from him. Thus, true rest is found in Jesus Christ our Saviour, who frees us from the tyranny of guilt, self and fear, and in Jesus Christ our Lord, when we submit to the authority of his teaching. For his yoke is easy, his burden is light, and he himself is 'gentle and humble in heart'.

Reflection questions from Tim Chester

1 What signs are there of an interest in freedom in the world around us? What signs are there among your family and friends?

2 What difference does it make to see sin not simply as specific misdeeds, but as self-centredness (a lack of love)? Can you identify ways in which we become enslaved by our self-centredness?

3 In which ways does fear prevent you from being the person you want to, or should, be?

4 In which ways is God constrained? In which sense is God free – more free than anyone else?

5 How would you describe the link Stott makes between freedom and love, in your own words?

6 What's the difference between freedom *from* authority and freedom *under* authority? Why is freedom under authority good news?

3

Christ and his cross

The gospel is good news of freedom, as we saw in the last chapter. Yet this on its own is a one-sided emphasis. For what the gospel announces, according to the New Testament, is not just what Christ offers people today, but what he once did to make this offer possible. The apostolic gospel brings together the past and the present, the once and the now, the historical event and the contemporary experience. It declares not only that Jesus saves, but also that he died for our sins, and was raised from death to accomplish that salvation. The gospel is not preached if the saving power is proclaimed and the saving events omitted, especially the cross.

In this chapter we will reflect on one of Paul's greatest statements about the origin, content and power of the gospel, and in particular about the centrality of Christ's cross.

> And so it was with me, brothers and sisters. When I came to you, I did not come with eloquence or human wisdom as I proclaimed to you the testimony about God. For I resolved to know nothing while I was with you except Jesus Christ and him crucified. I came to you in weakness with great fear and trembling. My message and my preaching were not with wise and persuasive words, but with a demonstration of the Spirit's power, so that your faith might not rest on human wisdom, but on God's power.[1]

From this essentially trinitarian text, three major lessons about evangelism stand out. They concern the Word of God, the cross of Christ and the power of the Spirit.

The Word of God

The gospel is truth from God. What Paul proclaimed to the Corinthians, he said, was not human wisdom, the wisdom of the world,[2] but the Word of God or the wisdom of God, which he here calls either God's 'testimony' or God's 'mystery'.[3] In other words, Paul's message came from God. The apostle's gospel is God's truth.

This is where all true evangelism must begin. We have not invented our message. We do not come to people with our own human speculations. Instead, we are bearers of God's Word, trustees of God's gospel, stewards of God's revealed secrets.

Moreover, Paul's delivery matched his message. He came to the Corinthians neither with 'eloquence' nor with 'human wisdom' (verse 1). As to content, he renounced proud human wisdom, humbly submitting instead to the Word of God about Christ (verse 2). As to delivery, he renounced proud human rhetoric, humbly relying instead on the Holy Spirit's power (verses 3–5). As C. H. Hodge put it in his commentary, he came 'neither as a rhetorician nor as a philosopher'.[4]

Please do not misinterpret this. There is no possible justification here either for a gospel without content or for a style without form. What Paul was renouncing was neither doctrinal substance nor rational argument, but only the wisdom and the rhetoric of the world. We know this because Luke tells us in Acts 18 what Paul's evangelistic ministry in Corinth had been like. First, 'Every Sabbath he reasoned in the synagogue, trying to persuade Jews and Greeks' (verse 4). Then he stayed on for eighteen months 'teaching them the word of God' (verse 11). Paul's own summary of his preaching was this: 'we try to persuade others.'[5] He both taught the truth and convinced people of the truth.

So we cannot invite people to come to Christ by closing, stifling or suspending their minds. No. Since God has made them rational beings, he expects them to use their minds. It is true that they will never believe apart from the illumination of the Spirit. Without the Spirit, all our arguments will be fruitless. 'But,' wrote Gresham Machen, 'because argument is insufficient, it does not follow that it is unnecessary. What the Holy Spirit does in the new birth is not to make a person a Christian regardless of the evidence, but on the contrary, to clear away the mists from his eyes and enable him to attend to the evidence.'[6]

So, then, the gospel is truth from God which has been committed to our trust. Our responsibility is to present it as clearly, coherently and cogently as we can and, like the apostles, to argue it as persuasively as we can. And all the time, as we do this, we will be trusting the Holy Spirit of truth to dispel people's ignorance, overcome their prejudices and convince them about Christ.

The cross of Christ

We come now to verse 2: 'I resolved to know nothing while I was with you except Jesus Christ and him crucified.' Some people misread this, as if Paul had written 'except Jesus Christ crucified', and conclude that his sole topic was the cross. What Paul actually wrote, however, was that he determined to know nothing 'except Jesus Christ' (his message focused on him) 'and [especially though not exclusively] him crucified'. It is this emphasis which is consistent with Luke's description in the Acts of Paul's evangelistic work. What about Christ's resurrection? It certainly loomed large in the preaching of the apostles. Yet they understood and proclaimed it, not as an isolated or independent event, but in relation to the cross. For the resurrection was not only the sequel to the death of Jesus; it was the reversal of the human verdict on him and the public vindication of the divine purpose in his death.

Before Paul arrived in Corinth, he made a decision to concentrate in his preaching on Christ, and especially on the cross. 'I decided' (RSV), he wrote, 'I determined' (AV), 'I resolved' (NEB, NIV) to do so.

It is this decision which we have to investigate. Why did he need to make it?

The popular reconstruction of what happened is well known. Paul arrived in Corinth from Athens. His sermon to the Athenian philosophers (so the theory goes) had been a flop. Not only had it been too intellectual, but Paul had not preached the gospel. He had focused on creation instead of the cross. As a result, there had been no conversions. So, on his way from Athens to Corinth, Paul repented of the distorted gospel he had preached in Athens and resolved in Corinth to limit his message to the cross.

I confess that when I first heard this theory many years ago now, I swallowed it hook, line and sinker. Since then, however, I have come to reject it, for it does not stand up to examination. First, Paul's Athens mission had not been a failure. On the contrary, 'Some of the people became followers of Paul and believed. Among them was Dionysius, a member of the Areopagus, also a woman named Damaris, and a number of others.'[7] Second, Luke in his account in Acts gives no hint that he thinks Paul's Athenian sermon was a mistake. On the contrary, he records it as a model of the apostle's preaching to Gentile intellectuals. Third, Paul almost certainly did preach the cross in Athens, since he proclaimed 'Jesus and the resurrection',[8] and you cannot preach the resurrection without the death which preceded it. It is true that, because of his Gentile audience, Paul began with idolatry and creation, rather than with Old Testament Scripture, but he did not stop there. The sermon Luke records would have taken only two minutes to preach; Paul must have elaborated this outline considerably. Fourth, Paul did not in fact change his tactics in Corinth. As in Athens, so in Corinth, Luke portrays him continuing to argue, to teach and to persuade.[9]

What was Paul's decision, then? Behind every resolute decision there lies some previous indecision, a situation in which various options present themselves and we are obliged to choose, deciding for one over against the alternatives. Evidently, then, behind Paul's decision to preach only Christ, and especially the cross, there lay a temptation, either to preach Christ without the cross, or not to preach Christ at all, but rather the wisdom of the world. So why was this a temptation to Paul as he travelled from Athens to Corinth? It was not surely his supposed failure in Athens, but rather his fear of the reception waiting for him in Corinth. So who were these Corinthians? Why was Paul so intimidated by them and so apprehensive as he approached them ('in weakness with great fear and trembling', verse 3)? Why did he need to make a firm decision as he prepared to engage with them?

As we answer these questions, we shall also uncover the chief contemporary objections to the message of Christ and his cross. Indeed, we shall see why we ourselves need to make the same resolute decision today.

(a) *The intellectual objection*, or the foolishness of the cross. Paul had already encountered intellectual scorn in Athens. The philosophers had insulted him by calling him a *spermologos* or 'seed-picker'. The word was applied literally to scavenging birds, and so to vagrants who lived on the scraps they could find in the gutter. Metaphorically, it denoted teachers who trade only in second-hand ideas. The Athenians worshipped at the shrine of originality.[10] They despised the old-fashioned and the obsolete.

The philosophers scoffed when the resurrection was mentioned.[11] 'They made fun of him' (GNT). I think that means they burst out laughing. How they reacted when Paul preached the cross, Luke does not say. But Paul knew that it was 'a stumbling-block to Jews and foolishness to Gentiles'.[12] To the unbelieving Jew it was inconceivable that the Messiah should die 'on a tree', that is, under the curse of God.[13] To the unbelieving Gentile it was ludicrous to suppose that a god, one of the immortals, should die. Celsus, the second-century cynic, was scathing in criticizing Christians for this. He imagined that in worshipping the one who, as Celsus put it, 'was taken prisoner and put to death', Christians are like people who worship the dead.[14]

Corinth had not escaped the intellectual arrogance of Athens. The two cities were only about fifty miles apart, as the crow flies. Paul's first letter to the Corinthians provides plenty of evidence that intellectual pride was one of the chief sins of the Corinthian church. This was the background against which Paul made his decision to renounce the wisdom of the world in favour of 'the foolishness of the cross'. Sneers and jeers awaited him. But he knew that 'the foolishness of God is wiser than man's wisdom'.[15]

Still today the message of the cross is deeply despised. The biblical, evangelical doctrine of the atonement (that Christ died the death we deserved to die instead of us as our substitute) is opposed and even mocked. It is said to be 'primitive', 'forensic', 'unjust', 'immoral' and 'barbaric'. A. J. Ayer called the allied Christian doctrines of sin and atonement 'intellectually contemptible and morally outrageous'.[16] A liberal theologian has described aspects of my own presentation in *The Cross of Christ* as 'untenable', 'unintelligible', 'not only inexplicable but also incomprehensible', and so 'incommunicable'. How are we to respond to this battery of negative epithets? We do not deny that some evangelical formulations have been unbalanced and unbiblical. Whenever we have cast Jesus Christ in the role of a third party who intervened to rescue us from an angry God, we have been guilty of a travesty which stands condemned. For it is God who loved the world and God who took the initiative to send his Son to die for us. Yet the initiative he took led to Christ being made to be 'sin' and 'a curse' for us,[17] and such language often arouses extraordinary hostility. Hence the temptation to trim the gospel of Christ crucified, to eliminate its more objectionable features, and to try to make it more palatable to sensitive modern palates. No wonder the apostle sounds almost fierce in expressing his decision to know only Jesus Christ and especially his cross. It was a choice between faithfulness and popularity.

(b) *The religious objection*, or the exclusiveness of the gospel. If Paul found Athens 'full of idols',[18] he is not likely to have found

Corinth less idolatrous. It is known to have had at least two dozen temples, each dedicated to a different deity. At the time of writing, seven massive pillars survive from the temple of Apollo in Corinth. And behind the city the rocky Acrocorinth rises nearly 2,000 feet (610 metres), on which the temple of Aphrodite once stood. So the Corinthians, like the Athenians, were 'very religious'.[19] They honoured many gods, who tolerated one another in amicable co-existence.

The Corinthians would not have raised any objection if the Christian evangelists were content to add Jesus to their already well-stocked pantheon of gods. But the apostle Paul had a very different object in view when he visited the city. He wanted Corinth, with all its inhabitants and all its gods, to bow down and worship Jesus. He came to Corinth with the firm intention of knowing nothing 'except Jesus Christ and him crucified'. He knew very well, as he wrote to them later, that there were 'many "gods" and many "lords"' who were competing for their allegiance. But, as far as he was concerned, 'there is but one God, the Father, from whom all things came and for whom we live; and there is but one Lord, Jesus Christ, through whom all things came and through whom we live'.[20] On this he was not prepared to compromise. He thought of his visit as having brought about their engagement to Christ, and he felt a godly jealousy for them. 'I promised you to one husband, to Christ, so that I might present you as a pure virgin to him,' he wrote. 'But I am afraid that just as Eve was deceived by the snake's cunning, your minds may somehow be led astray from your sincere and pure devotion to Christ.'[21] For Jesus Christ would not share his glory with Apollo or Aphrodite or anybody else.

The world's religious situation has not greatly changed. True, the old gods of Greece and Rome have long since been discredited and discarded. But new gods have arisen in their place, and other ancient faiths have experienced a resurgence. As a result of the internet, social media and ease of travel, many countries are increasingly pluralistic. What people want is an easy-going syncretism, a truce in inter-religious competition, a mishmash of the best from all religions. But we Christians cannot surrender either the finality or the uniqueness of Jesus Christ. There is simply nobody else like him. His incarnation, atonement and resurrection have no parallels. As a result, he is the one and only mediator between God and humanity.[22] This exclusive affirmation is strongly, even bitterly, resented. It is regarded by many as intolerably intolerant. Yet the claims of truth compel us to maintain it, however much offence it may cause.[23]

(c) *The personal objection*, or the humbling of human pride. Common to all religions except Christianity is the flattering notion (expressed in different ways) that we are capable, if not of achieving our salvation, at least of contributing substantially to it. This doctrine of self-salvation is exceedingly conducive to our self-esteem. It appeals to our proud ego. It saves us from the ultimate embarrassment of being humbled before the cross.

The Corinthians were no exception – they were a proud people. They were proud of their city, which had been beautifully rebuilt by Julius Caesar in 46 BC, following its destruction a century before. They were proud that Augustus had promoted Corinth over Athens as the capital of the new province of Achaia. They were proud of their trade, their affluence, their culture, their Isthmian games and their religious zeal.

Then along came this brash Christian missionary, this whipper-snapper, this ugly little fellow with a bald head, bandy legs and heavy brows, who appeared to have no respect for their distinguished city. He presumed to tell them that neither their wisdom, nor their wealth, nor their religion could save them. There was nothing they could do to save themselves from the judgment of God – or even help towards their salvation. This was why Jesus Christ had died for them, and apart from him they would perish. Who did he think he was to insult them in this way? It was a stunning humiliation to a proud people. The message of the cross was a stumbling-block to proud Jews and proud Gentiles alike. No wonder the main response to the gospel in Corinth came from the lower ranks of society: 'Not many of you were wise by human standards; not many were influential; not many were of noble birth.' Instead, it was the foolish, the weak, the lowly and the despised, who knew they had nothing to offer, whom God chose and called.[24]

Still today nothing keeps people out of the kingdom of God more than pride. As Emil Brunner put it, in all other religions 'man is spared the final humiliation of knowing that the Mediator (Jesus Christ) must bear the punishment instead of him ... He is not stripped absolutely naked.'[25] But the gospel strips us naked (we have no clothing in which to appear before God), and declares us bankrupt (we have no currency with which to buy the favour of heaven).

(d) *The moral objection*, or the call to repentance and holiness. Corinth was a flourishing commercial centre, with trade routes both north and south by land, and east and west by sea. So the city was full of merchants, travellers and sailors. Being strangers in a strange city, they exercised little moral restraint. Besides, Aphrodite, the goddess of love who held court in her temple above the city, encouraged sexual promiscuity among her devotees, and provided a thousand prostitutes to roam the city's streets by night. Corinth was the Vanity Fair of the ancient world. The Greeks even turned the name of the city into a verb, 'to corinthianize' (*korinthiazomai*). It meant 'to practise immorality'.

A brazenly immoral city like Corinth could hardly be expected to welcome the gospel, with its summons to repentance, its warnings that the sexually depraved will not inherit God's kingdom,[26] and its insistence that after justification comes sanctification (growth in holiness), and after sanctification glorification (when evil will be abolished).

The modern world has no more time for the gospel's call to self-control than had the ancient world. It likes to say that there are no such things as moral absolutes any longer, that sexual morality is only a matter of social custom, that restraint is bad while permissiveness is good, and that Christianity with its prohibitions is the enemy of freedom.

(e) *The political objection*, or the lordship of Jesus Christ. There was a lot of political fervour – even fanaticism – in the Roman Empire. Loyal Roman procurators tended to encourage it, and acted ruthlessly to put down any attempt at rebellion. We need to remember that Jesus himself was condemned in a Roman court for the political offence of sedition, for claiming to be a king and rival to Caesar. Similarly, Paul and Silas were accused in Philippi of 'advocating customs unlawful for us Romans to accept or practise',[27] while in Thessalonica they were said to be 'defying Caesar's decrees, saying that there is another king, one called Jesus'.[28]

Were these charges true or untrue? They were both. Of course, neither Jesus nor the apostles ever stirred up armed rebellion against Rome. They were not zealots, the first-century equivalent of terrorists. But they did proclaim that Jesus had ushered in God's kingdom, that his kingdom took precedence over all lesser loyalties, that it would spread throughout the world, and that the king was coming back to take his power and reign. It sounded positively seditious. Indeed, it *was* seditious if 'sedition' means denying undisputed authority to the state by according it to God's Christ.

Still today the one thing a totalitarian regime cannot endure is for people to refuse to give it the total allegiance which it covets. Christians submit conscientiously to the state, insofar as its God-given authority is used to promote good and punish evil. But we will not worship it. It is Christ we worship, to whom all authority in heaven and on earth has been given. Christ died and rose in order to be Lord of all.

Here, then, are five objections which are levelled against the gospel of Christ and his cross, and which Paul expected to encounter in Corinth. He knew that his message of Christ crucified would be regarded as

- intellectually foolish (incompatible with wisdom);
- religiously exclusive (incompatible with tolerance);
- personally humiliating (incompatible with self-esteem);
- morally demanding (incompatible with freedom);
- politically subversive (incompatible with patriotism).

No wonder Paul felt weak and nervous so that he trembled with fear.[29] No wonder he recognized that he had to make a decision. On the one hand, it was a negative decision to renounce the wisdom of the world, namely every system that is offered as an alternative to the gospel. On the other hand, it was a positive decision to proclaim nothing but Jesus Christ, and especially his cross. The same alternative faces us today. It is the choice between the wisdom of the world, which is foolishness to God, and the foolishness of the cross, which is the wisdom of God.

The power of the Spirit

Some contemporary Christians, hearing Paul's confession of weakness, fear and trembling, would doubtless have rebuked him. 'Paul,' they might have said, 'you've no business to feel nervous or afraid. Pull yourself together! Don't you know what it is to be filled with the Spirit? You ought to be strong, confident and bold.'

But Paul was not afraid to admit that he was afraid. To be sure, he had a mighty intellect and a strong personality, and these powers he had dedicated to Christ. But he was also physically weak and emotionally vulnerable. According to tradition, his appearance was unprepossessing. His critics said that 'in person he is unimpressive and his speaking amounts to nothing'.[30] So he was nothing much to look at or to listen to. In addition, disease of some kind (his so-called 'thorn in the flesh'[31]) seems to have affected his eyesight and even disfigured his face.[32] And he knew the unpopularity of his gospel, the opposition it would arouse in Corinth, and so the cost of being faithful to it.

In what, then, did he put his trust? He tells us in 1 Corinthians 2:4–5. His confidence was not in 'wise and persuasive words' (NIV) or 'plausible words of wisdom' (RSV). That is, he relied neither on the wisdom nor on the eloquence of the world. Instead of the world's wisdom, he preached Christ and his cross (verses 1–2), and instead of the world's rhetoric, he trusted in the powerful demonstration which the Holy Spirit gives to the Word. For only the Holy Spirit can convince people of their sin and need, open their eyes to see the truth of Christ crucified, bend their proud wills to submit to him, set them free to believe in him, and bring them to new birth. This is the powerful 'demonstration' which the Holy Spirit gives to words spoken in human weakness.

This theme of 'power through weakness' is a vital element in Paul's Corinthian correspondence. In both letters the apostle emphasizes that it is through human weakness that divine power operates best. He hints that God deliberately makes and keeps his people weak in order to show that the power is his.[33] Paul even adds that this principle applies to God himself, for it is through his own weakness in the cross that he puts forth his power to save.

In 1 Corinthians 1 and 2, the same theme of power through weakness is repeated in three variations:

- First, we have a weak and foolish message – the message of Christ and the cross (1:18–25).
- Second, it is proclaimed by weak and foolish preachers (2:1–5).
- Third, it is welcomed by weak and foolish people (1:26–31).

Thus, God chose a weak instrument (Paul) to bring a weak message (the cross) to weak people (the Corinthian working classes). Why? It was 'so that no one may boast before him', and so that he who does boast will 'boast in the Lord' alone.[34]

The first five verses of 1 Corinthians 2 are perhaps the noblest and richest statement on evangelism in the New Testament. They tell us that the gospel is truth from God about Christ and his cross in the power of the Spirit. Thus, the gospel is not human speculation, but divine revelation; not popular wisdom, but Christ and his despised cross; not by the pressures of advertisement or personality, but by the Holy Spirit. The gospel comes from God, focuses on Christ and him crucified, and is authenticated by the Holy Spirit. This is the trinitarian evangelism of the New Testament.

Reflection questions from Tim Chester

1 How might we be tempted to rely on eloquence or human wisdom in our evangelism?
2 We should not rely on eloquence or human wisdom, but neither should we be boring or irrational. Which is the correct way to approach sharing the message of the gospel?
3 Stott says people find the message of Christ crucified (1) intellectually foolish, (2) religiously exclusive, (3) personally humiliating, (4) morally demanding and (5) politically subversive. Think of times when you have faced hostility as you have told people about Jesus or invited them to church. Can you link that hostility to one of these reasons?
4 Pick one of these reactions to Christ crucified. How could you respond in a way that commends Christ?
5 What should we do when evangelism fills us with fear and trembling?
6 'God chose a weak instrument (Paul) to bring a weak message (the cross) to weak people (the Corinthian working classes).' How does God use these three weaknesses to display his grace and power?

4

The relevance of the resurrection

The most outrageous of all Christian claims is that Jesus Christ rose from the dead. It strains our credulity to the limit. Human beings have used all their ingenuity to defy or deny death. But only Christ has claimed to conquer it – to defeat it in his own experience and deprive it of its power over others. 'I am the resurrection and the life,' he declared. 'The one who believes in me will live, even though they die; and whoever lives by believing in me will never die.'[1] Again, 'I am the Living One; I was dead, and now look, I am alive for ever and ever! And I hold the keys of [i.e. have authority over] death and Hades.'[2]

The very first Christians already shared this confidence. This is clear both from their brave, and even joyful, readiness to die for Christ, and from the earliest preaching of the apostles. Soon after Pentecost Luke tells us that the Jewish authorities in Jerusalem 'were greatly disturbed because the apostles were . . . proclaiming in Jesus the resurrection of the dead'.[3] The heart of their sermons follows the same pattern: 'you killed him, God raised him, and we are witnesses.'[4] And Paul did not deviate from this,[5] so that the Athenian philosophers, listening to him in the market-place, concluded that he was advocating two foreign deities, because they heard his repeated references to *Iēsous* (Jesus) and *anastasis* (resurrection).[6] When Paul came to pass on to the Corinthians an outline of the original gospel he had himself received, he concentrated, 'as of first importance', on the death, burial, resurrection and appearances of Jesus.[7] Those earliest followers of Jesus seem to have been both clear and confident about his resurrection.

Three major questions are raised by the claim that Jesus rose (or was raised) from the dead. First, what does it mean (a question of semantics)? Second, did it really happen (a question of history)? Third, is it important (a question of relevance)?

What does the resurrection mean?

Before we decide whether the resurrection of Jesus was a real historical event, we need to be sure we agree what is meant by 'resurrection'. David Jenkins, a former Bishop of Durham, for example, claimed to believe in the resurrection. 'I do believe in the resurrection of Jesus Christ from the dead,' he told his Diocesan Synod. 'Anyone who says that I do not believe in the resurrection . . . is a liar.' But what he understood by resurrection was very different from the understanding of the New Testament. For Dr Jenkins did not believe that the resurrection involved the transformation of the body of Jesus. Indeed, he caricatured this view as 'a conjuring trick with bones'.

What is meant in the Creed by the resurrection of Jesus Christ? How should we think of the risen Lord? It may be helpful if we clarify what we do not believe, before coming on to affirm what we do.

First, the risen Lord is not just *a surviving influence*. We are not to think of him as merely surviving death, like a ghost. 'Look at my hands and my feet,' he said. 'It is I myself! Touch me and see; a ghost does not have flesh and bones, as you see I have.'[8] Neither does 'resurrection' mean the mere survival of an influence. Many leaders, who during their lifetime captured the hearts of their contemporaries, live on after death in the sense that the memory of their example is a continuing inspiration.

This was certainly true of Che Guevara. He had an extraordinary following. Sartre once described him as 'the most complete man of his age'. In his thirty-nine years (before he was killed in the jungle) he had been a doctor, an author, an economist, a banker, a political theorist and a guerrilla fighter. He became a legend during his lifetime, a folk hero. In every Cuban classroom the children would chant, 'We will be like Che.' And after his death his influence became greater still. He provided Marxists with the image of a secular saint and martyr. For years the walls of Latin American student buildings were chalked with the words, 'Che lives!'[9]

It was the same when Archbishop Makarios of Cyprus died in August 1977. His followers spray-painted public buildings with the words, 'Makarios lives!'

Is this all Christians mean when they say that 'Jesus lives'? Some people seem to be saying little more than this, namely that Jesus continues to exert his power and spread his love in the world. Others are affirming some kind of continuing, personal existence for Jesus, so that 'he walks with me and talks with me along life's narrow way'. Yet the grand affirmation of the New Testament is not 'he lives', but that 'he is risen'. The resurrection becomes an experience for us only because it was first an event that actually introduced a new order of reality.

Second, the risen Lord is not *a resuscitated corpse*. To 'resuscitate' can mean either to revive a patient who has gone into a coma or to bring someone back to life who has been pronounced clinically dead. In this second sense Jesus performed three resuscitations during his public ministry. He 'raised from death' (i.e. restored to this life) the daughter of Jairus, the son of the widow of Nain, and Lazarus. Each of these three was dead, but was brought back to this life by Jesus. One understands the sympathy that C. S. Lewis expressed for Lazarus: 'To be brought back and have all one's dying to do again was rather hard.'[10]

But Jesus' own resurrection was not a resuscitation in either sense. On the one hand, he was not revived from a swoon or coma, for he had been dead for about thirty-six hours. On the other hand, he was not brought back to this life with the need to die again. Yet it is popularly supposed that this is what Christians believe about 'resurrection', namely that the body is miraculously reconstituted out of the identical particles of which it is at present composed, and that it then resumes this vulnerable and mortal life. But, no, Jesus was raised to a new plane of existence, in which he was now no longer mortal but 'alive for ever and ever'.[11] Whatever popular notions some people may have entertained, the faith of the church has never seen the risen Lord either as a rather ethereal ghostly influence or as a resuscitated corpse.

Third, the risen Lord is not *a revived faith* in the experience of his disciples. This was the 'demythologized' reconstruction of Rudolf Bultmann, the New Testament scholar. He began by declaring that the resurrection of Jesus was 'obviously . . . not an event of past history'. Why was this so obvious to him? Because 'an historical fact which involves a resurrection from the dead is utterly inconceivable'. But since the church in every age seems to have had little difficulty in conceiving what Bultmann pronounced inconceivable, what was his problem? It lay in the 'incredibility of a mythical event like the resuscitation of a corpse – for that is what the resurrection means'. What is truly incredible, however, is not the resurrection of Jesus, but the misunderstanding of Bultmann who confused it with a resuscitation.

How then did Bultmann interpret the 'myth' of Jesus' resurrection? In this way: 'if the event of Easter Day is in any sense an historical event additional to the event of the cross, it is nothing else than the rise of faith in the risen Lord . . . All that historical criticism can establish is the fact that the first disciples came to believe in the resurrection.' In other words, Easter was not an event, but an experience; not the objective, historical resurrection of Jesus from the dead, but a subjective, personal recovery of faith in the hearts and minds of his followers.[12]

Fourth, the risen Lord is not just *an expanded personality*. This seems to express what David Jenkins believes. He wrote, 'The resurrection means that God acted to establish Jesus in his person, in his achievements and in his continuing effect.'[13] Declaring his conviction that Jesus 'rose from the dead', he explained this by saying that 'the very life and power and purpose and personality which was in him was actually continuing . . . in the sphere of history, so that he was a risen and living presence and possibility'.[14] Elsewhere, Jenkins has spoken of the resurrection as an 'explosion' of the personality of Jesus. So the resurrection was a kind of event, even though it did not involve his body. Dr Jenkins believes in the 'risenness' and 'livingness' of Jesus, though his personality is not now embodied (except in the church).

Fifth, the risen Lord is not merely *a living experience of the Spirit*. In his book *The Structure of Resurrection Belief*, Peter Carnley, the former Anglican Archbishop of Perth, Western Australia, says we should think of the resurrection as a present experience rather than a past event. We should think of it as an experience of the Spirit. In his opening chapter he makes plain his sceptical stance. He asserts that Paul nowhere alludes to the empty tomb, even in 1 Corinthians 15:3–8, and that the so-called appearances were not objective. He argues that *ōphthē* ('he appeared') means not so much perception through sight (a visible appearance) as the reception of a new revelation (an intellectual apprehension), or at most a mixture of the two, with the emphasis on the second.[15]

Next come three long chapters in which Archbishop Carnley urges that there was, in fact, no after-death event. The real Easter event was the disciples' coming to faith.[16] Consequently, from chapter 5 onwards he refers no longer to 'the resurrection' (an event) but to 'the raised Christ' (an experience). For the Easter faith 'involves a post-mortem experience of encounter with the raised Christ', who is known as the Spirit.[17] And the way we come to recognize the true Spirit of Jesus is that he continues to manifest in the Christian fellowship the same self-giving love which he displayed on the cross.[18] But, ingenious as this reconstruction is, it does not do justice to the data of the New Testament, as we shall see.

Sixth, and in contrast to the previous five proposals, the risen Lord is *a transformed person*. The evidence presented in the Gospels is that Jesus is the same person with the same identity before and after the resurrection. 'It is I myself,' he says in Luke 24:39. But the resurrection gave him a transformed, transfigured, glorified body. The resurrection was a dramatic act of God by which he stopped the natural process of decay and decomposition,[19] rescued Jesus out of the realm of death, and changed his body into a new vehicle for his personality, endowed with new powers and possessing immortality.

Belief in resurrection means belief in bodily resurrection. This is the message of 1 Corinthians 15. This great chapter is in two parts, the first relating to the *fact* of the resurrection (verses 1–34), and the second to the *nature* of the resurrection (verses 35–58). In the first part the resurrection appearances of Jesus appear to be physical, but in the second part the body is said to be 'sown a natural body' (or 'physical body', RSV) and 'raised a spiritual body' (verse 44). How, then, are we to harmonize the two halves of 1 Corinthians 15 with each other? Some scholars seize on the expression 'a spiritual body' and insist that the resurrection appearances of verses 5–8 must be understood in the light of this term. But in the light of the New Testament as a whole, we should approach the issue the other way round. In other words, the nature of the 'spiritual body' must be interpreted in a way that does not contradict the evidence that the resurrected Jesus had a physical body. This evidence for this is found not only in the Gospel narratives of the empty tomb, but in the first sermons of Peter and in the early verses of 1 Corinthians 15. I will focus on the latter.

In Paul's statement of the gospel, which he claims to be both the *original* gospel (which he had himself 'received', verse 3) and the *universal* gospel (which they and he all believed, verse 11), he made four affirmations, namely that 'Christ died . . . that he was buried, that he was raised on the third day . . . and that he appeared.' Two aspects of the resurrection of Jesus are clear from this.

First, it was *an objective, historical event*. Indeed, it was datable: it happened 'on the third day'. David Jenkins has called it 'not an event, but a series of experiences'. But no, it became a series of experiences only because it was first an event. The words 'on the third day' witness to the historicity of Jesus' resurrection, much as the words 'under Pontius Pilate' in the Apostles' Creed witness to the historicity of his sufferings and death.

Second, the resurrection was *a physical event*. It involved his body. The four verbs (died, was buried, was raised, appeared) all have the same subject, namely 'Christ', as a historical, physical person. This is beyond question in the case of the first two. It was his body that died and his body that was buried. The natural presumption, then, is that the very same historical, physical Christ is the subject of the third and fourth verbs, namely that he was raised and then appeared. It would take a high degree of mental gymnastics to claim that, without warning, the subject changes in the middle of the sentence, that although his body died and was buried, only his personality was raised and seen, so that he was raised while still remaining buried. No, since it was his body that was buried, it must have been his body that was raised. This probably explains the mention of his burial in some of the early apostolic sermons.[20] It is entirely gratuitous, in the light of this, to maintain that the apostle Paul was ignorant of the empty tomb.

It is true that when the dead and buried body of Jesus was 'raised', it was changed in the process. We are envisaging neither a resuscitation (in which he was raised bodily, but not changed), nor a survival (in which he was changed into a ghost, but not raised bodily at all), but a resurrection (in which he was both raised and changed simultaneously).

Did the resurrection really happen?

Let us grant that the apostles, including Paul, did believe in a literal, datable, physical resurrection and transformation of Jesus. Were they correct? Can we, who live in the sophisticated, contemporary world of astrophysics, microbiology and computer science, also believe in the resurrection? Yes, we can and we should. Many millions do.

Several books have been written to marshal the evidence for the resurrection.[21] This is an important part of Christian apologetics. All I can attempt here is a straightforward summary of the main lines of evidence.

First, there is *the disappearance of the body.* Everybody agrees that Joseph's tomb was empty, even those who deny the Gospel writers' stories. The rumours of resurrection could never have gained credence if people could have visited the tomb and found the body still in position. So the body had gone. The question has always been, 'What became of it?' No satisfactory explanation has been given of its disappearance, except for the resurrection.

We cannot accept that Jesus only fainted on the cross, then revived in the tomb, and subsequently came out of it by himself. For one thing, both the centurion and then Pilate assured themselves that Jesus was dead. For another, when he did emerge, he gave people the impression that he had conquered death, not that he had almost been conquered by it and was now a seriously sick man in need of hospital treatment.

So did the authorities (Roman or Jewish) deliberately remove the body, in order to prevent the disciples from spreading the rumour that he had risen? It is hard to believe this, since, when the apostles began to proclaim 'Jesus and the resurrection',[22] the authorities could have immediately scotched the new movement by producing the body, instead of which they resorted to violence.

In this case, did the disciples steal the body as part of a hoax, in order to deceive people into thinking that he had risen? That is an impossible theory, for they were prepared to suffer and die for the gospel, and people are not willing to become martyrs for a lie that they have themselves perpetrated.

No explanation of the empty tomb holds water except that God had raised Jesus from the dead.

Second, there is *the reappearance of the Lord.* Not only did Jesus' body disappear from the tomb, but Jesus then kept *reappearing* during a period of nearly six weeks. He is said to have showed himself to certain individuals (e.g. Mary Magdalene, Peter and James), to the Twelve, both with and without Thomas, and on one occasion 'to more than five hundred of the brothers and sisters at the same time', most of whom were still alive when Paul wrote about this in about AD 54,[23] and could therefore have been cross-examined.

These resurrection appearances cannot be dismissed as inventions, since it is plain beyond doubt that the apostles really believed that Jesus had risen. The stories had not been made up. But nor were they hallucinations. Tough fishermen like Peter, James and John are not the kind of personalities who might be susceptible to such symptoms of mental disorder. Furthermore, the variety of times, places, moods and people in regard to the appearances, together with people's initial reaction of unbelief, make the theory of wishful thinking untenable. The only alternative to inventions and hallucinations is valid, objective appearances.

Third, there is *the emergence of the church.* Something happened to change the apostles and to send them out on their mission to the world. When Jesus died, they were heartbroken, confused and frightened. But within less than two months they came out of hiding, full of joy, confidence and courage. What can account for this dramatic transformation? Only the resurrection, together with Pentecost which followed soon afterwards. From that bunch of disillusioned nobodies has grown a universal community numbering one third of the population of the world. It would take a lot of credulity, even of cynicism, to believe that the whole Christian edifice had been built on the lie of a resurrection that never happened.

The disappearance of the body, the reappearance of the Lord and the emergence of the church together constitute a solid foundation for believing in the resurrection.

Why is the resurrection important?

What we have to ask about the resurrection is not only whether or not it happened, but whether it really matters that it happened. For if it happened, it happened nearly 2,000 years ago. How can an event that took place so long ago have any great importance for us today? Why on earth do Christians make such a song and dance about it? Is it not irrelevant? No, I believe the resurrection resonates with our human condition. It speaks to our needs as no other distant event does or could. It is the mainstay of Christian assurance.

First, the resurrection of Jesus assures us of *God's forgiveness*. We have already seen that forgiveness is one of our most basic needs and one of God's best gifts. The head of a large English mental hospital has been quoted as saying, 'I could dismiss half my patients tomorrow if they could be assured of forgiveness.'[24] We all have a skeleton or two in some dark cupboard, memories of things of which in our better moments we are thoroughly ashamed. Our conscience nags, condemns, torments us.

Several times during his public ministry, Jesus spoke words of forgiveness and peace. In the upper room he described the communion cup as his 'blood of the covenant . . . poured out for many for the forgiveness of sins'.[25] Thus, he linked our forgiveness with his death. And since throughout Scripture death is always welded to sin as its just desert ('the wages of sin is death'),[26] he can have meant only that he was going to die the death that we deserved, to die in our place, in order that we might be spared and forgiven.

That is what he said. But how can we know that he was right, that he achieved by his death what he said he would achieve? How can we know that God accepted his death in our place as 'a full, perfect, and sufficient sacrifice, oblation, and satisfaction, for the sins of the whole world' (as the Book of Common Prayer puts it)? The answer is that, if he had remained dead, if he had not been visibly and publicly raised from death, we would never have known. Indeed, without the resurrection we would have to conclude that his death was a failure. The apostle Paul saw this logic clearly: 'If Christ has not been raised, our preaching is useless and so is your faith.' Again, 'if Christ has not been raised, your faith is futile; you are still in your sins. Then those also who have fallen asleep in Christ are lost.'[27] The terrible consequences of no resurrection would be that the apostles are false witnesses, believers are unforgiven, and the Christian dead have perished. But in fact, Paul continued, Christ was raised from the dead. And by raising him, God has assured us that he approves of his sin-bearing death, that he did not die in vain, and that those who trust in him receive a full and free forgiveness. The resurrection validates the cross.

Second, the resurrection of Jesus assures us of *God's power*. For we need God's power in the present as well as his forgiveness of the past. Is God really able to change human nature, which appears to be so intractable? Can he really make cruel people kind, selfish people unselfish, immoral people self-controlled, and bitter people sweet? Is he able to take people who are dead to spiritual reality, and make them alive in Christ? Yes, he really is! He is able to give life to the spiritually dead, and to transform us into the likeness of Christ.

But these are great claims. Can they be substantiated? Only because of the resurrection. Paul prays that the eyes of our heart may be enlightened, so that we may know 'his incomparably great power for us who believe'. And to help us grasp the measure of this power, not only does God give us an inward illumination by his Spirit, but he has given us an outward, public, objective demonstration of it in the resurrection. For the power available for us today is the very power which 'he exerted when he raised Christ from the dead'.[28] In this way the resurrection is portrayed as the supreme evidence in history of the creative power of God.

We are always in danger of trivializing the gospel, of minimizing what God is able to do for us and in us. We speak of becoming a Christian as if it were no more than turning over a new leaf, making a few superficial adjustments to our usual patterns of behaviour, and becoming a bit more religious. Then scratch the surface, crack the veneer, and behold, underneath we are still the same old pagans, unredeemed and unchanged. But no, becoming and being a Christian according to the New Testament is something much more radical than this. It is a decisive act of God. It is nothing less than a resurrection from the death of alienation and self-centredness, and the beginning of a new and liberated life. In a word, the same God of supernatural power who raised Jesus from physical death can raise us from spiritual death. And we know he can raise *us* because we know he raised *him*.

Third, the resurrection of Jesus assures us of *God's ultimate triumph*. One of the major differences between the religions and ideologies of the world lies in their vision of the future. Some offer no hope, but sink into existential despair. Bertrand Russell, when still a young man of thirty, expressed his conviction that

> no fire, no heroism, no intensity of thought and feeling, can preserve an individual life beyond the grave; that all the labours of the ages, all the devotion, all the inspiration, all the noonday brightness of human genius, are destined to extinction in the vast death of the solar system, and that the whole temple of man's achievement must inevitably be buried beneath the debris of a universe in ruins.[29]

Others think of history more in circular than in linear terms, as an endless cycle of reincarnations, with no release but the non-existence of nirvana. Marxists continue to promise Utopia on earth, but the vision has lost credibility. Secular humanists dream of taking control of their own evolution. But insofar as this involves genetic manipulation, the dream degenerates into a nightmare.

Christians, on the other hand, are confident about the future, and our Christian 'hope' (which is a sure expectation) is both individual and cosmic. Individually, apart from Christ, the fear of personal death and dissolution is almost universal. The comedian and film-maker Woody Allen typifies this terror. It has been an obsession with him. True, he can still joke about it. 'It's not that I'm afraid to die,' he once quipped; 'I just don't want to be there when it happens.'[30] But mostly he is filled with dread. In an article in *Esquire* he said, 'The fundamental thing behind *all* motivation and *all* activity is the constant struggle against annihilation and against death. It's absolutely stupefying in its terror, and it renders anyone's accomplishments meaningless.'[31]

Jesus Christ, however, rescues his disciples from this horror. We will not only survive death, but be raised from it. We are to be given new bodies like his resurrection body,[32] with new and undreamed-of powers.[33] For he is called both the 'firstfruits' of the harvest[34] and 'the firstborn from the dead'.[35] Both metaphors give the same assurance. He was the first to rise; all his people will follow. We will have a body like his. 'Just as we have borne the likeness of the earthly man [Adam] so shall we bear the likeness of the man from heaven [Christ].'[36]

Our hope for the future, however, is also cosmic. We believe that Jesus Christ is going to return in spectacular glory to bring history to its fulfilment in eternity. He will not only raise the dead, but regenerate the universe.[37] He will make all things new.[38] The whole creation is going to be set free from its present bondage to decay and death. The groans of nature are the labour pains which promise the birth of a new world.[39] There is going to be a new heaven and a new earth, which will be the home of righteousness.[40]

So the living hope of the New Testament is impressively 'material' for both the individual and the cosmos. The individual believer is promised not just survival, not even immortality, but a resurrected, transformed body. And the destiny of the cosmos is not an ethereal 'heaven', but a re-created universe.

Is there any evidence, however, for this amazing assertion that both we and our world are to be totally renewed? Yes, the resurrection of Jesus is the basis of both expectations. It provides solid, visible, tangible, public evidence of God's purpose to complete what he has begun, to redeem nature, to give us new bodies in a new world. As Peter expressed it, God 'has given us new birth into a living hope through the resurrection of Jesus Christ from the dead'.[41] For the resurrection of Jesus was the beginning of God's new creation. It is not enough to believe that the personality, presence and power of Jesus live on. We need to know that his body was raised. For the resurrection body of Jesus was the first bit of the material order to be redeemed and transfigured. It is the divine pledge that one day the rest will be redeemed and transfigured.[42]

Thus the resurrection of Jesus assures us of God's forgiveness, power and ultimate triumph. It enables us

- to face our past (however many reasons we have to be ashamed of it), confident of God's forgiveness through him who died for our sins and was raised;
- to face our present (however strong our temptations or heavy our responsibilities), confident of the sufficiency of God's power;
- to face our future (however uncertain it may be), confident of God's final triumph of which the resurrection is the pledge.

The resurrection, precisely because it was a decisive, public, visible act of God within the material order, brings us firm assurance in an otherwise insecure world.

Reflection questions from Tim Chester

1 What is the difference between a resuscitated corpse and a resurrected body? What difference does this make to our hope?
2 What do you think is the appeal of reducing the resurrection to a surviving influence, a resuscitated corpse, a revived faith, an expanded personality or a living experience?
3 What is the problem with these approaches?
4 Which process or factors led you to believe in the physical resurrection of Jesus (if you do)? How might your answer help you respond to sceptical friends?
5 When might you use the truth of the resurrection to provide comfort in a pastoral situation?
6 Stott says, 'Our hope for the future . . . is also cosmic.' What difference should this cosmic hope make in day-to-day life?

5

Jesus Christ is Lord

The apostolic gospel went beyond the fact and significance of the cross and resurrection, to their purpose: 'For to this end Christ died and lived again, that he might be Lord both of the dead and of the living.'[1]

It is well known that the earliest, shortest, simplest of all Christian creeds was the affirmation 'Jesus is Lord'. Those who acknowledged his lordship were baptized and received into the Christian community. For it was recognized, as Paul wrote, on the one hand that 'if you declare with your mouth, "Jesus is Lord," and believe in your heart that God raised him from the dead, you will be saved',[2] and on the other that 'no-one can say, "Jesus is Lord," except by the Holy Spirit'.[3]

It may at first sight seem extraordinary that two Greek words, *Kyrios Iēsous* or 'Lord Jesus' (for there is no connecting verb in either of the two verses quoted in the previous paragraph), could possibly be a satisfactory basis for identifying and welcoming somebody as a genuine Christian. Are they not hopelessly inadequate? Is this not theological reductionism at its worst?

The answer to these questions is 'no'. For the two words concerned, which sound like a minimal Christian confession, are pregnant with meaning. They have enormous implications for both Christian faith and Christian life. In particular, they express both a profound theological conviction about the historic Jesus and therefore a radical personal commitment to him. This conviction and this commitment are the subjects of this chapter.

Theological conviction

Perhaps the best way to investigate the doctrinal overtones of calling Jesus 'Lord' is to take a fresh look at Philippians 2:9–11. These verses form the climax of what is sometimes called *Carmen Christi*, 'the song of Christ'. For Paul is probably quoting an early Christian hymn about Christ. In doing so, he gives it his apostolic seal of approval. He affirms that Christ, although he shared God's nature and enjoyed equality with him, emptied himself of his glory and humbled himself to serve, becoming obedient even to death on a cross (verses 6–8). Paul continues:

> Therefore God exalted him to the highest place
> and gave him the name that is above every name,
> that at the name of Jesus every knee should bow,
> in heaven and on earth and under the earth,
> and every tongue acknowledge that Jesus Christ is Lord,
> to the glory of God the Father.
> (verses 9–11)

As a Christian hymn, used by the church and endorsed by the apostle, it indicates how the early Christians thought of Jesus. Three points stand out.

First, *Paul gave Jesus a God-title*. That is, Paul referred to Jesus as 'Lord'. It is true, of course, that *kyrios* was used with different meanings in different contexts. Sometimes it meant no more than 'sir', as when Mary Magdalene thought the risen Jesus was the gardener[4] or when the priests asked Pilate to have the tomb made secure.[5] But when used by Jesus' disciples in relation to him, *kyrios* was more than a polite form of address. It was a title, as when they called him 'the Lord Jesus' or 'the Lord Jesus Christ'. The meaning becomes clear against the background of the Old Testament.

When the Old Testament came to be translated into Greek in Alexandria around 200 BC, the devout Jewish scholars did not know how to handle the sacred name Yahweh or Jehovah. They were too reticent to pronounce it; they did not feel free to translate or even to transliterate it. So they put the paraphrase *ho kyrios* ('the Lord') instead, which is why 'Yahweh' still appears in most English versions as 'the LORD'.

What is truly amazing is that the followers of Jesus – knowing that in Jewish circles *ho kyrios* was the traditional title for Yahweh, Creator of the universe and covenant God of Israel – nevertheless chose to apply the same title to Jesus. They did not see any anomaly in this, even though it was tantamount to saying that 'Jesus is God'.

Second, *Paul transferred to Jesus a God-text*. In Isaiah 45:23 Yahweh had said of himself,

> By myself I have sworn,
> my mouth has uttered in all integrity
> a word that will not be revoked:
> Before me every knee will bow;
> by me every tongue will swear.

Now Paul, or the hymn-writer he is quoting, has the audacity to lift this text out of Isaiah and reapply it to Jesus. The implication is unavoidable. The honour, which the prophet said was due to Yahweh, the apostle says is due to Christ. And it is an honour which is universal, involving 'every knee' and 'every tongue'.

A similar example is the New Testament use of Joel 2:32. The prophet had written that 'everyone who calls on the name of the LORD [i.e. God] will be saved'. On the Day of Pentecost, however, Peter reapplied this promise to Jesus, urging his hearers to believe in Jesus and be baptized in his name.[6] Similarly, Paul wrote later that the Lord Jesus 'is Lord of all and richly blesses all who call on him, for, "Everyone who calls on the name of the Lord will be saved."'[7]

Thus, the saving power of Yahweh to Israel has become the saving power of Jesus to Jewish and Gentile believers alike.

Third, *Paul demanded for Jesus God-worship*. Paul says every knee will bow before Jesus in worship. Prayer is regularly addressed to Jesus in the New Testament, especially when Paul links 'God our Father' and 'our Lord Jesus Christ' as together being the source of grace and the object of prayer.[8] One is reminded too of Hebrews 1:6: 'Let all God's angels worship him.' It is assumed in the New Testament that grace flows from Christ and that worship is due to him. Indeed, Christolatry (the worship of Christ) preceded Christology (the developed doctrine of Christ). But Christolatry is idolatry if Christ is not God. Athanasius saw this clearly in the fourth century. He faced the heresy of Arianism, which claimed Christ was merely a created being. One of the ways Athanasius countered this was to point to the long-established practice of worshipping Jesus.

Here, then, are three important data contained in the Christian hymn Paul was quoting. The early Christians gave Jesus a God-title ('Lord'), transferred to him God-texts (regarding the salvation he grants and the honour he deserves) and offered him God-worship (the bowed knee). These facts are incontrovertible, and they are all the more impressive for being uncontrived and almost casual.

It is also significant that the New Testament writers did not argue the rightness of making the daring identification that Jesus is God, for there was no need for them to do so. Paul fiercely defended the gospel of justification by grace through faith because it was being challenged. But he did not debate the divine lordship of Jesus, which must mean it was not being disputed. So already, within a few years of the death and resurrection of Jesus, his deity was part of the universal faith of the church.

The confession that 'Jesus is Lord' has a second theological inference, namely that he is Saviour as well as God. There is a tradition in some evangelical circles to distinguish sharply between

Jesus the Saviour and Jesus the Lord, and even to suggest that conversion involves trusting him as Saviour without necessarily surrendering to him as Lord. The motive behind this teaching is good, namely to safeguard the truth of justification by faith alone and not introduce self-salvation by the back door. Nevertheless, this position is biblically indefensible. Not only is Jesus 'our Lord and Saviour', one and indivisible, but his lordship implies his salvation and actually announces it. That is, his title 'Lord' is a symbol of his victory over all the forces of evil, which have been put under his feet. The very possibility of our salvation is due to this victory. It is precisely because he is Lord that he is also able to be Saviour.[9] There can be no salvation without lordship. The two affirmations 'Jesus is Lord' and 'Jesus saves' are virtually synonymous.

Radical commitment

The word *kyrios* or 'Lord' could be used, as we have seen, as no more than a respectful term of address. But it was most commonly used of owners, whether of land, property or slaves. Possession carried with it full control and the right of disposal. It is with this understanding that Paul, Peter and James began their letters by calling themselves 'slave of Jesus Christ'. They knew that he had bought them at the cost of his own blood, and as a result they belonged to him and were entirely at his service.

This personal ownership by Christ, and commitment to Christ, is to penetrate every part of the lives of his disciples. It has at least six dimensions.

First, it has *an intellectual dimension*. I begin with our mind because it is the central citadel of our personality and effectively rules our lives. Yet it is often the last stronghold to capitulate to the lordship of Jesus. The truth is that we rather like to think our own thoughts and vent our own opinions. And if they conflict with the teaching of Jesus, so much the worse for him!

But Jesus Christ claims authority over our minds. 'Take my yoke upon you and learn from me,' he said.[10] His Jewish hearers will immediately have understood him. For they commonly spoke of 'the yoke of Torah' (the law), to whose authority they submitted. Now Jesus spoke of *his* teaching as a yoke. His followers were to become his pupils, to subject themselves to his instruction, and to learn from him. Nor need they be afraid of this. For on the one hand, he was himself 'gentle and humble in heart', and on the other, his yoke was 'easy'. Under its light discipline they would find 'rest' for their souls. In other words, true 'rest' is found under Christ's yoke (not in resisting it), and true freedom is found under his authority (not in discarding it). The apostle Paul was later to write something similar, when he expressed his resolve to 'take captive every thought to make it obedient to Christ'.[11]

Contemporary Christians may be anxious to respond sensitively to the challenges of the modern world, but we cannot jettison the authority of Jesus Christ to do so. Disciples have no liberty to disagree with their divine teacher. What we believe about God, about humanity, male and female, made in God's image, about life and death, duty and destiny, Scripture and tradition, salvation and judgment, and much else besides, we have learned from him. There is an urgent need in our day, in which wild and weird speculations abound, to resume our rightful position at his feet. 'Only the person who follows the command of Jesus without reserve,' wrote Dietrich Bonhoeffer, 'and submits unresistingly to his yoke, finds his burden easy, and under its gentle pressure receives the power to persevere in the right way. The command of Jesus is hard, unutterably hard, for those who try to resist it. But for those who willingly submit, the yoke is easy and the burden is light.'[12]

Second, radical commitment to Jesus Christ has *a moral dimension.* All round us today moral standards are slipping. People doubt whether there are any moral absolutes left. Relativism has permeated the world and is seeping into the church.

Even some evangelical believers misrepresent Scripture on the subject of the law. They quote the apostle Paul's well-known statements that 'Christ is the end of the law'[13] and 'you are not under the law',[14] turn a blind eye to their context, and misinterpret them as meaning that the category of law has now been abolished. As a result, they suppose we are no longer under obligation to obey it and are instead free to disobey it. But Paul meant something quite different. He was referring to the way of salvation, not the way of holiness. He was insisting that for our acceptance with God we are 'not under law but under grace', since we are justified by faith alone, not by works of the law. But we are still under the moral law for our sanctification. As Luther kept saying, the law drives us to Christ to be justified, but Christ sends us back to the law to be sanctified.

The apostle is quite clear about the place of the law in the Christian life. He insists that both the atoning work of Christ and the indwelling presence of the Spirit have in view obedience to the law. Why did God send his Son to die for our sins? Answer: 'in order that the righteous requirements of the law might be fully met in us, who . . . live . . . according to the Spirit'.[15] And why has God put his Spirit in our hearts? Answer: in order to write his law there.[16] God's Old Testament promise of the new covenant could be expressed as 'I will put my law in their minds and write it on their hearts'[17] and 'I will put my Spirit in you and move you . . . to keep my laws'.[18]

So Jesus Christ calls us to obedience. 'Whoever has my commands and keeps them is the one who loves me. The one who loves me will be loved by my Father, and I too will love them and show myself to them.'[19] The way to prove our love for Christ is neither by loud protestations of loyalty like Peter, nor by singing sentimental songs in church, but by obeying his commandments. The test of love is obedience, Jesus said, and the reward of love is a self-revelation of Christ.

Third, Christian commitment has *a vocational dimension*. That is to say, it includes our life work. To say 'Jesus is Lord' commits us to a lifetime of service. Every single Christian is called to ministry; indeed, we are all called to give our lives in ministry. If this strikes you as extraordinary, it is probably because you are thinking of 'ministry' in terms of ordained pastoral ministry. But pastoral ministry is only one of many ministries. My point is that we are all called to ministry or service of some kind. The reason it is possible to say this is that we are followers of one who assumed 'the very nature of a servant',[20] insisted that he had 'not come to be served, but to serve',[21] and added, 'I am among you as one who serves.'[22] If we claim to follow Jesus, therefore, it is inconceivable that we should spend our lives in any way other than in service.

This means we must be able to see our job or profession in terms of service. Our daily work is meant to be a major sphere in which Jesus exercises his lordship over us. Beyond and behind our earthly employer we should be able to discern our heavenly Lord. Then we will be 'working for the Lord, not for human masters', since 'it is the Lord Christ [we] are serving'.[23]

In November 1940 the city of Coventry was devastated by aerial bombardment, including its fourteenth-century cathedral. After the war the ruins of the old cathedral were preserved, while a new cathedral was built beside it. From medieval times the old cathedral had around its walls a series of guild chapels (e.g. for the smiths, the drapers, the mercers and the dyers), symbolizing the close link between the church and these trades. These chapels were destroyed, but in their place 'hallowing places' have been set round the ruined walls, expressing the implications of the prayer, 'Hallowed be your name':

In industry, God be in my hands and in my making.
In the arts, God be in my senses and in my creating.
In the home, God be in my heart and in my loving.
In commerce, God be at my desk and in my trading.

In healing, God be in my skill and in my touching.
In government, God be in my plans and in my deciding.
In education, God be in my mind and in my growing.
In recreation, God be in my limbs and in my leisure.

Fourth, the lordship of Christ has *a social dimension*. This means that the followers of Jesus have social as well as individual responsibilities, for example, to family, firm, neighbourhood, country and world. But it means more than this.

There is a sense in which to confess 'Jesus is Lord' is to acknowledge him as Lord of society, even of those societies or segments of society that do not explicitly acknowledge his lordship. Consider this dilemma which the New Testament sets before us. On the one hand, we are told that Jesus is Lord. He has dethroned and disarmed the principalities and powers, triumphing over them in the cross.[24] God has exalted him to his right hand and put everything under his feet.[25] As a result, he can claim that all authority has been given to him.[26] On the other hand, we continue to struggle against the principalities and powers of darkness. They may have been defeated, even deprived of power, but they are still active, influential and unscrupulous.[27] The apostle John even goes so far as to declare that 'the whole world is under the control of the evil one'.[28] In fact, this dilemma is well summed up in Psalm 110:1, which was quoted by Jesus and several New Testament writers:

The LORD says to my lord:
'Sit at my right hand
until I make your enemies
a footstool for your feet.'

Within the compass of this one verse the Messiah is depicted both as *reigning* at God's right hand and as *waiting* for the overthrow of his enemies.

71

How can we reconcile these two perspectives? Is Jesus Lord, or is Satan? Is Christ reigning over his enemies, or waiting for them to surrender? The only possible answer to these questions is 'both'. We have to distinguish between what is *de jure* (by right) and what is *de facto* (in fact or reality). *De jure* Jesus is Lord, for God has exalted him to the highest place. *De facto*, however, Satan rules, for he has not yet conceded defeat or been destroyed.

How does this tension affect our discipleship? Because Jesus is Lord by right, that is, by divine appointment, we cannot settle for any situation that denies it. We long that he who is Lord should be acknowledged as Lord. This is our evangelistic task. But even in a society which does not specifically acknowledge his lordship, we are still concerned that his values prevail, that human rights and human dignity be accorded to people of all races and religions, that honour be given to women and children, that justice be secured for the oppressed, that society become more just, compassionate, peaceful and free. Why? Why do we care about these things? Because Jesus is Lord of society by right, and because he cares about them. This is not to resurrect the old 'social gospel' of theological liberalism, which made the mistake of identifying a caring society with the kingdom of God. It is rather to take seriously the truth that Jesus is Lord of society and therefore to seek to make it more pleasing to him.

It was during his inaugural address at the opening of the Free University of Amsterdam in 1880 that Abraham Kuyper, who was later to become Prime Minister of the Netherlands, said, 'There is not one inch in the entire area of human life about which Christ, who is Sovereign of all, does not cry out "Mine!"' Similarly, Dr David Gill of New College, Berkeley, has written, 'Jesus is Lord not just of the inner life, afterlife, family life and church life, but of intellectual life, political life – all domains.'[29]

Fifth, a radical commitment to Christ has *a political dimension*. We need to remember that Jesus was condemned for both a political and a religious offence. In the Jewish court he was found guilty of blasphemy because he called himself the Son of God. But in the Roman court he was condemned for sedition because he called himself a king, and Rome recognized no king but Caesar. Thus, the claims of Jesus had inescapable political implications. His statement that we are to 'give back to Caesar what is Caesar's and to God what is God's' may have been deliberately enigmatic.[30] But it certainly implied that there are areas over which God is Lord and into which Caesar may not intrude.

The early Christians faced a continuing conflict between Christ and Caesar. During the first century the emperors manifested ever-increasing megalomania. They had temples erected in their honour and demanded divine homage from their subjects. These claims came into direct collision with the lordship of Christ, whom Christians honoured as king,[31] indeed as 'the ruler of the kings of the earth'.[32] Pliny, the early second-century governor of Bithynia, described in a letter to the Emperor Trajan how he brought before him in court those Christians he suspected of disloyalty, and how he discharged only those who 'offered invocation with wine and frankincense to your [i.e. the Emperor's] image'.[33] But how could believers say 'Caesar is Lord' when they had confessed that 'Jesus is Lord'? They went to prison and death rather than deny the lordship of Christ.

The deification of the state did not end with the Roman Empire. Still today there are totalitarian regimes which demand from their citizens an unconditional allegiance that Christians cannot possibly give. The disciples of Jesus are to respect the state, and within limits submit to it. But they will neither worship it, nor give it the uncritical support it desires. As a result, discipleship sometimes calls for disobedience. Indeed, civil disobedience is a biblical doctrine, for there are four or five notable examples of it in Scripture.[34] It arises naturally from the affirmation that Jesus is Lord. The principle is clear, even though its application may involve believers in agonies of conscience. It is this. We are to submit to the state, because its authority is derived from God and its officials are God's ministers,[35] right up to the point where obedience to the state would involve us in disobedience to God. At that point our Christian duty is to disobey the state in order to obey God. For if the state misuses its God-given authority, and presumes either to command what God forbids or to forbid what God commands, then we have to say 'no' to the state in order to say 'yes' to Christ. As Peter put it, 'We must obey God rather than human beings!'[36] Or in Calvin's words, 'obedience to man must not become disobedience to God.'[37]

In 1957 Hendrik Verwoerd, then Minister of Native Affairs in South Africa, announced the 'Native Laws Amendment Bill'. It contained a 'church clause', which would have prevented any association of different ethnic groups in 'church, school, hospital, club or any other institution or place of entertainment'. The Archbishop of Cape Town at the time was a gentle scholar called Geoffrey Clayton. He decided, with his bishops, albeit with reluctance and apprehension, to disobey. He wrote to the Prime Minister to say that if the Bill were to become law, he would be 'unable to obey it or to counsel our clergy and people to do so'. The following morning he died, perhaps under the pain and strain of threatened civil disobedience. The Bill was amended, but in a mischievous way which would have penalized the black worshippers rather than the church leaders. After it became law, a letter was read out in every Anglican church, calling on the clergy and people to disobey it.

Sixth, commitment to Christ has *a global dimension*. To affirm 'Jesus is Lord' is to acknowledge his universal lordship. For, according to Philippians 2:9, God has 'highly exalted'. The word Paul uses occurs nowhere else in the New Testament, and may even have been coined by Paul. It is *hyperypsoō*, which could translate as 'super-exalted'. It means God raised Jesus 'to the loftiest heights'.[38] And God's purpose in doing so was that every knee should bow to him and every tongue confess him Lord. We have no liberty to place any limitation on the repeated word 'every'. Therefore, if it is God's desire that everybody acknowledge Jesus, it must be our desire as well. Hindus speak of 'the Lord Krishna' and Buddhists of 'the Lord Buddha', but we cannot accept these claims. Only Jesus is Lord. He has no rivals.

There is no greater incentive to world mission than the lordship of Jesus Christ. Mission is neither an impertinent interference in other people's private lives, nor a dispensable option which may be rejected. It is an unavoidable deduction from the universal lordship of Jesus Christ.

The two-word affirmation *Kyrios Iēsous* sounded pretty harmless at first hearing. But we have seen that it has far-reaching ramifications. Not only does it express our conviction that Jesus is God and Saviour, but it also indicates our radical commitment to him. The dimensions of this commitment are

- intellectual (bringing our minds under Christ's yoke);
- moral (accepting his standards and obeying his commands);
- vocational (spending our lives in his liberating service);
- social (seeking to penetrate society with his values);
- political (refusing to idolize any human institution);
- global (being jealous for the honour and glory of his name).

Reflection questions from Tim Chester

1 Stott argues that confessing Jesus is Lord involves recognizing he is the 'LORD', Creator of the universe and covenant God of Israel. What are the implications for our attitude to Jesus? What are the implications for our understanding of God?

2 When are you aware of the teaching of Christ contrasting with the thinking of our culture?

3 What is your attitude to God's law as a guide for our sanctification (becoming more like Jesus)? Does your attitude need to change?

4 We are to work as though 'working for the Lord' in our offices,
  factories, workshops, warehouses, classrooms and homes. What
  are some of the concrete differences this makes in your life?
5 When might obeying Christ require us to disobey the state?
6 How does the lordship of Christ propel us out in mission?
  What might this mean for you?

Conclusion
The now and the not yet

I began in the Introduction with the tension between the 'then' (past) and the 'now' (present); I end with another tension, between the 'now' (present) and the 'not yet' (future). These two tensions belong together. For it is in and through Jesus Christ that the past, the present and the future are brought into a creative relationship. Christians live in the present, but do so in thankfulness for the past and in anticipation of the future.

As I conclude this book, I'm going to focus on balanced biblical Christianity. Balance is a rare commodity these days in almost every sphere, not least among us who seek to follow Christ.

One of the things about the devil is that he is a fanatic, and the enemy of all common sense, moderation and balance. One of his favourite pastimes is to tip Christians off balance. If he cannot get us to *deny* Christ, he will get us to *distort* Christ instead. As a result, lopsided Christianity is widespread, in which we overemphasize one aspect of a truth, while underemphasizing another.

A balanced grasp of the now–not yet tension would be very beneficial for Christian unity, and especially to a greater harmony among evangelical believers. We may agree on the doctrinal and ethical fundamentals of the faith. Yet we seem to be constitutionally prone to quarrelling and dividing, or simply to going our own way and building our own empires.

Kingdom come and coming

Fundamental to New Testament Christianity is the perspective that we are living 'in between times' – between the first and the second comings of Christ, between kingdom come and kingdom coming.

The theological basis for this tension is to be found in Jesus' own teaching about the kingdom of God. Everyone accepts both that the kingdom featured prominently in his teaching and that he announced its coming. Where scholars have disagreed, however, is over the time of its arrival. Has the kingdom already come, because Jesus brought it with him? Or is its coming still in the future, so that we await it expectantly? Or does the truth lie between these positions?

Albert Schweitzer is an example of a scholar who thought that, according to Jesus, the kingdom lay entirely in the future. As an apocalyptic prophet, Jesus taught (mistakenly) that God was about to intervene supernaturally and establish his kingdom. The radical demands he made on his disciples were an 'interim ethic' in the light of the imminent arrival of the kingdom. Schweitzer's position is known as 'thoroughgoing' or 'consistent' eschatology.

At the opposite extreme was C. H. Dodd, with his belief that the coming of the kingdom is wholly in the past (known as 'realized eschatology'). He laid a heavy emphasis on two verses whose verbs are in the perfect tense, namely 'The kingdom of God has arrived'[1] and 'The kingdom of God has come upon you'.[2] Dodd concluded that there is no future coming of the kingdom, and that passages which speak of one were not part of Jesus' own teaching.

In place of these extreme polarities, most scholars have taken a middle position – that Jesus spoke of the kingdom as both a present reality and a future expectation.

Jesus clearly taught that the time of fulfilment had arrived;[3] that 'the strong man' was now bound and disarmed, enabling the plundering of his goods, as was evident from his exorcisms;[4] that the kingdom was already either 'within' or 'among' people;[5] and that it could now be 'entered' or 'received'.[6]

Yet the kingdom was a future expectation as well. It would not be perfected until the last day. So he looked forward to the end, and taught his disciples to do so also. They were to pray 'Your kingdom come'[7] and to 'seek' it first,[8] giving priority to its expansion. At times he also referred to the final state of his followers in terms of 'entering' the kingdom[9] or 'receiving' it.[10]

One way in which the Bible expresses the tension between the 'now' and the 'not yet' is in the terminology of the two 'ages'. From the perspective of the Old Testament, history is divided between 'this present age' and 'the last days', namely the kingdom of righteousness to be introduced by the Messiah.[11] This simple structure of two consecutive ages was decisively changed, however, by the coming of Jesus. For he brought in the new age, and died for us in order to deliver us 'from the present evil age'.[12] As a result, the Father has already 'rescued us from the dominion of darkness and brought us into the kingdom of the Son he loves'.[13] We have even been raised from death and seated with Christ in the heavenly realm.[14]

At the same time, the old age persists. So the two ages overlap. 'The darkness is passing and the true light is already shining.' One day the old age will be terminated (which will be 'the end of the age'),[15] and the new age, which was introduced with Christ's first coming, will be brought about at his second. Meanwhile, the two ages continue, and we are caught in the tension between them. We are summoned not to 'conform to the pattern of this world', but rather to 'be transformed' according to God's will and to live consistently as children of the light.[16]

Nevertheless, the tension remains: we have already *been* saved, yet also we *shall* be saved one day.[17] And we are already God's adopted children, yet we also are waiting for our adoption.[18] Already we have 'crossed over from death to life', yet eternal life is also a future gift.[19] Already Christ is reigning, although his enemies have not yet become his footstool.[20]

Caught between the present and the future, the characteristic stance of Christians is variously described as hoping,[21] waiting,[22] longing[23] and groaning,[24] as we wait both 'eagerly'[25] and also 'patiently'.[26]

The essence of the interim period between the 'now' and the 'not yet' is the presence of the Holy Spirit in the people of God. On the one hand, the gift of the Spirit is the distinctive blessing of the kingdom of God and the principal sign that the new age has dawned.[27] On the other, because his indwelling is only the beginning of our kingdom inheritance, it is also the guarantee that the rest will one day be ours. The New Testament uses three metaphors to illustrate this. The Holy Spirit is the 'firstfruits', pledging that the full harvest will follow,[28] the 'deposit' or first instalment, pledging that the full payment will be made,[29] and the foretaste, pledging that the full feast will one day be enjoyed.[30]

Here are some examples of the tension between the 'now' and the 'not yet'.

Revelation, holiness and healing

The first example is in *the intellectual sphere*, or the question of *revelation*.

We affirm with joyful confidence that God has revealed himself to human beings, not only in the created universe, in our reason and our conscience, but supremely in his Son Jesus Christ, and in the Bible's witness to him. We dare to say that we know God, because he has himself taken the initiative to draw aside the curtain, which would otherwise hide him from us. We rejoice greatly that his Word throws light on our path.[31]

But we do not yet know God as he knows us. Our knowledge is partial because his revelation has been partial. He has revealed everything which he intends to reveal, and which he considers to be for our good, but not everything that there is to reveal. There are many mysteries left, and so 'we live by faith, not by sight'.[32]

We should take our stand alongside those biblical authors who, although they knew themselves to be agents of divine revelation, nevertheless confessed humbly that their knowledge remained limited. Even Moses, 'whom the LORD knew face to face', acknowledged, 'O Sovereign LORD, you have only [RSV] begun to show to your servant your greatness and your strong hand.'[33] Then think of the apostle Paul, who likened his knowledge both to the immature thoughts of a child and to the distorted reflections of a mirror.[34]

So, then, although it is right to glory in the givenness and finality of God's revelation, it is also right to confess our ignorance of many things. We know and we don't know. 'The secret things belong to the LORD our God, but the things revealed belong to us and to our children for ever, that we may follow all the words of this law.'[35] It is very important to maintain this distinction. Speaking personally, I would like to see more boldness in our proclaiming what has been revealed, and more reticence about what has been kept secret. Agreement in plainly revealed truth is necessary for unity, even while we give each other freedom in secondary matters. And the way to recognize these is when Christians who are equally anxious to be submissive to Scripture nevertheless reach different conclusions about them. I am thinking, for example, about controversies over baptism, church government, liturgy and ceremonies, claims about spiritual gifts, and the fulfilment of prophecy.

The second tension is in *the moral sphere*, or the question of *holiness*.

God has already put his Holy Spirit within us, in order to make us holy.[36] The Holy Spirit is actively at work within us, subduing our fallen, selfish human nature and causing his fruit to ripen in our character.[37] Already, we can affirm, he is transforming us into the image of Christ.[38]

But our fallen nature has not been eradicated, for 'the flesh desires what is contrary to the Spirit',[39] so that 'if we claim to be without sin, we deceive ourselves'.[40] We have not yet become completely conformed to God's perfect will, for we do not yet love God with all our being, or our neighbour as ourselves. As Paul put it, we have not 'already become perfect' (GNT), but we 'press on towards the goal', confident that 'he who began a good work in [us] will carry it on to completion until the day of Christ Jesus'.[41]

So, then, we are caught in a painful tension between the 'now' and the 'not yet', between dismay over our continuing failures and the promise of ultimate freedom. On the one hand, we must take God's command, 'Be holy because I . . . am holy'[42] and Jesus' instruction, 'Go, and do not sin again'[43] with the utmost seriousness. On the other hand, we have to acknowledge the reality of indwelling sin alongside the reality of the indwelling Spirit.[44] The sinless perfection we long for continues to elude us.

The third tension between the 'already' and the 'not yet' is to be found in *the physical sphere* or the question of *healing*.

We affirm that the long-promised kingdom of God broke into history with Jesus Christ, who was not content merely to *proclaim* the kingdom but went on to *demonstrate* its arrival by the extraordinary things he did. His power was especially evident in the human body as he healed the sick, expelled demons and raised the dead.

He also gave authority to both the Twelve and the Seventy to extend his mission in Israel, and to perform miracles. How much wider he intended his authority to go is a matter of dispute. Generally speaking, miracles were 'the signs of a true apostle'.[45] Nevertheless, it would be foolish to attempt to limit or domesticate God. We must allow him his freedom and his sovereignty, and be entirely open to the possibility of physical miracles today.

But God's kingdom has not yet come in its fullness. For 'the kingdom of the world' has not yet 'become the kingdom of our Lord and of his Christ' when 'he will reign for ever and ever'.[46] In particular, our bodies have not yet been redeemed, and nature has not yet been entirely brought under Christ's rule.

So we have to recognize the 'already'–'not yet' tension in this sphere too. To be sure, we have 'tasted . . . the powers of the coming age',[47] but so far it has been only a taste. Part of our Christian experience is that the resurrection life of Jesus is 'revealed in our mortal body'.[48] At the same time, our bodies remain frail and mortal. To claim perfect health now would be to anticipate our resurrection. The bodily resurrection of Jesus was the pledge, and indeed the beginning, of God's new creation. But God has not yet uttered the decisive word, 'I am making everything new!'[49] Those who dismiss the very possibility of miracles today forget the 'already' of the kingdom, while those who expect them as what has been called 'the normal Christian life' forget that the kingdom is 'not yet'.

Church and society

Fourth, the same tension is experienced in *the ecclesiastical sphere*, or the question of *church discipline.*

Jesus the Messiah is gathering round him a people of his own, a community characterized by the truth, love and holiness to which he has called it. But Christ has not yet presented his bride to himself 'as a radiant church, without stain or wrinkle or any other blemish, but holy and blameless'.[50] On the contrary, her present life and witness are marred by error, discord and sin.

So, then, whenever we think about the church, we need to hold together the ideal and the reality. The church is both committed to truth and prone to error, both united and divided, both pure and impure. Not that we are to accept its failures. We are to cherish the vision of both the doctrinal and ethical purity and the visible unity of the church. We are called to 'fight the good fight of the faith',[51] and to 'make every effort to keep the unity of the Spirit through the bond of peace'.[52] And in pursuit of these things there is a place for discipline in cases of serious heresy or sin.

And yet error and evil are not going to be eradicated completely from the church in this world. They will continue to coexist with truth and goodness. 'Let both grow together until the harvest,' Jesus said in the parable of the wheat and the weeds.[53] Neither the Bible nor church history justifies the use of severe disciplinary measures in an attempt to secure a perfectly pure church in this world.

The fifth area of tension between the 'now' and the 'then', the 'already' and the 'not yet', is *the social sphere*, or the question of *progress*.

We affirm that God is at work in human society. This is partly in his 'common grace', as he gives the world the blessings of family and government, by which evil is restrained and relationships are ordered. And it is also through the members of his redeemed community, who penetrate society like salt and light, making a difference by hindering decay and dispelling darkness.

But God has not yet created the promised 'new heaven and . . . new earth, where righteousness dwells'.[54] There are still 'wars and rumours of wars'.[55] Swords have not yet been beaten into ploughshares and spears into pruning hooks.[56] The nations have not yet renounced war as a method of settling their disputes. Selfishness, cruelty and fear continue.

So, then, although it is right to campaign for social justice and to expect to improve society further, we know that we shall never perfect it. Although we know the transforming power of the gospel and the wholesome effects of Christian salt and light, we also know that evil is ingrained in human nature and human society. Only Christ at his second coming will eradicate evil and enthrone righteousness for ever.

Here, then, are five areas (intellectual, moral, physical, ecclesiastical and social) in which it is vital to preserve the tension between the 'already' and the 'not yet'.

Three types of Christian

There are three distinct types of Christian, according to the extent to which they manage to maintain this biblical balance.

First, there are *the 'already' Christians* who emphasize what God has already given us in Christ. But they give the impression that, in consequence, there are now no mysteries left, no sins that cannot be overcome, no diseases that cannot be healed, and no evils that cannot be eradicated. In short, they seem to believe that perfection is attainable now.

Their motives are blameless. They want to glorify Christ – so they refuse to set limits to what he is able to do. But their optimism can easily degenerate into presumption and end up in disillusion. They forget the 'not yet' of the New Testament, and that perfection awaits the second coming of Christ.

Second, there are *the 'not-yet' Christians* who emphasize the incompleteness for the time being of the work of Christ and look forward to the time when he will complete what he has begun. But they seem to be preoccupied with our human ignorance and failure, the pervasive reign of disease and death, and the impossibility of securing either a pure church or a perfect society.

Their motive is excellent too. If the 'already' Christians want to glorify Christ, the 'not-yet' Christians want to humble sinners. They are determined to be true to the Bible in their emphasis on our human depravity. But their pessimism can easily degenerate into complacency; it can also lead to acceptance of the status quo and to apathy in the face of evil. They forget the 'already' of what Christ has done by his death, resurrection and gift of the Spirit – and of what he can do in our lives, and in church and society, as a result.

Third, there are *the 'already–not-yet' Christians*. They want to give equal weight to the two comings of Jesus. On the one hand, they have great confidence in the 'already', in what God has said and done through Christ. On the other hand, they exhibit a genuine humility before the 'not yet', humility to confess that the world will remain fallen and half-saved until Christ perfects at his second coming what he began at his first.

It is this combination of the 'already' and the 'not yet' which characterizes authentic biblical evangelicalism, and which exemplifies the balance that is so urgently needed today.

Our position as 'contemporary Christians' rests securely on the person of Jesus, whose death and resurrection belong to the 'already' of the past, and whose glorious second coming to the 'not yet' of the future. As we acclaim in faith and triumph:

Christ has died!
Christ is risen!
Christ will come again!

Notes

Preface

1 Revelation 1:8.
2 Hebrews 13:8.

Series introduction: the Contemporary Christian – the then and the now

1 Psalm 119:105; cf. 2 Peter 1:19.
2 Dietrich Bonhoeffer, *Letters and Papers from Prison*, enlarged edn (SCM Press, 1971), p. 279.
3 Matthew 11:19.
4 See Jaroslav Pelikan, *Jesus Through the Centuries* (Yale University Press, 1985), pp. 182–193.
5 2 Corinthians 11:4.
6 2 Timothy 1:15; cf. 4:11, 16.
7 Acts 26:25.
8 Ezekiel 2:6–7.

1 The human paradox

1 J. S. Whale, *Christian Doctrine* (1941; Fontana, 1957), p. 33.
2 Ibid., p. 41.
3 Genesis 1:26–28.
4 Keith Thomas, *Man and the Natural World: Changing Attitudes in England 1500–1806* (1983; Penguin, 1984).
5 Ibid., p. 31.
6 Ibid., p. 31.
7 Ibid., p. 32. See also pp. 37–39, 43, 166 and 177.
8 Genesis 1:26, 28; Psalm 8:5–8.
9 Genesis 2:7; 7:22.
10 Genesis 1:22, 28.

11 Psalms 73:22; 32:9.

12 Isaiah 1:3.

13 Jeremiah 8:7.

14 Proverbs 6:6–8.

15 Genesis 2:8, 15.

16 Genesis 3:8–9.

17 John 17:21.

18 Emil Brunner, *Man in Revolt* (1937; ET Lutterworth, 1939), pp. 419–420.

19 Act II, Scene 2.

20 Mark 7:14–15, 21–23.

21 Matthew 7:11.

22 Dag Hammarskjöld, *Markings*, translated by Leif Sjöberg and W. H. Auden (Faber, 1964), pp. 128–129.

23 Mark 7:23.

24 Exodus 3:1–6; Isaiah 6:1–6; Ezekiel 1, especially verse 28.

25 C. S. Lewis, *Prince Caspian* (Geoffrey Bles, 1951), p. 185.

26 Richard Holloway at the Catholic Renewal Conference in Loughborough, April 1978.

27 See 2 Peter 3:13.

2 Authentic freedom

1 Daniel Halpern, 'A Sort of Exile in Lyme Regis', *London Magazine*, March 1971.

2 Luke 4:18–19, quoting Isaiah 61:1–2.

3 John 8:36.

4 Galatians 5:1.

5 Mark Twain, *Following the Equator* (1897), Vol. 1, ch. 27.

6 Cf. Psalm 130:4.

7 John 8:31–34.

8 Philippians 3:10.

9 Ephesians 1:22.

10 Michael Ramsey, *Freedom, Faith and the Future* (SPCK, 1970), p. 12.

11 E.g. Hebrews 6:18; James 1:13; Habakkuk 1:13.

12 2 Timothy 2:13 (rsv).

13 Morris West, *Children of the Sun* (1957; Pan, 1958), pp. 94–95.

14 The interview appeared in *Le Monde*, and in an English translation in the *Guardian Weekly* on 23 June 1985.

15 Mark 8:35.

16 Matthew 11:28–30.

3 Christ and his cross

1 1 Corinthians 2:1–5.

2 1 Corinthians 1:20–21.

3 See 1 Corinthians 2:7.

4 C. H. Hodge, *The First Epistle to the Corinthians* (1857; Banner of Truth, 1959), p. 29.

5 2 Corinthians 5:11; cf. Acts 18:13.

6 J. Gresham Machen, *The Christian Faith in the Modern World* (1936; Eerdmans, 1947), p. 63.

7 Acts 17:34.

8 Acts 17:18.

9 For a fuller refutation of the popular reconstruction, see my *The Message of Acts* in the Bible Speaks Today series (IVP, 1990), pp. 289–290.

10 Acts 17:18, 21.

11 Acts 17:32.

12 1 Corinthians 1:23.

13 Galatians 3:13 (rsv).

14 Origen, *Against Celsus*, III. 34.

15 1 Corinthians 1:25.

16 The *Guardian Weekly*, 30 August 1979.

17 2 Corinthians 5:21; Galatians 3:13.

18 Acts 17:16.

19 Acts 17:22.

20 1 Corinthians 8:5–6.

21 2 Corinthians 11:2–3.

22 1 Timothy 2:5.

23 For more on this topic, see ch. 1 of John Stott, *The World* (IVP, 2019).

24 1 Corinthians 1:26–29.

25 Emil Brunner, *The Mediator* (1927; Westminster, 1947), p. 474.

26 1 Corinthians 6:9–10.

27 Acts 16:21.

28 Acts 17:7.

29 1 Corinthians 2:3 (NEB).

30 2 Corinthians 10:10.

31 2 Corinthians 12:7.

32 E.g. Galatians 4:13–14.

33 See *hina* ('in order that') in 2 Corinthians 4:7 and 12:9–10.

34 1 Corinthians 1:29–31.

4 The relevance of the resurrection

1 John 11:25–26.

2 Revelation 1:18.

3 Acts 4:2.

4 E.g. Acts 2:23–24, 32; 3:13–15; 5:30–32.

5 E.g. Acts 13:28–31.

6 Acts 17:18.

7 1 Corinthians 15:3–8.

8 Luke 24:39.

9 See Andrew Sinclair, *Guevara* (Fontana, 1970), especially pp. 70 and 88.

10 W. H. Lewis (ed.), *Letters of C. S. Lewis* (Geoffrey Bles, 1966), p. 307.

11 Revelation 1:18.

12 Rudolf Bultmann, *Kerygma and Myth* (1941; ET SPCK, 1953), pp. 38–42.

13 David Jenkins, *Living with Questions* (SCM Press, 1969), pp. 138–139. See also the critique by J. Murray Harris, entitled *Easter in Durham* (Paternoster, 1985).

14 From the television programme *Credo* in April 1984.

15 Peter Carnley, *The Structure of Resurrection Belief* (Clarendon Press, 1987), p. 17f.

16 Ibid., p. 164.

17 Ibid., pp. 200, 266.

18 Ibid., p. 368.

19 Acts 2:27.

20 E.g. Acts 2:23–32; 13:28–31, 37.

21 See e.g. Frank Morison, *Who Moved the Stone?* (Faber, 1930); J. N. D. Anderson, *The Evidence for the Resurrection* (IVP, 1950); Stuart Jackman, *The Davidson File* (Lutterworth, 1982); E. M. B. Green, *The Day Death Died* (IVP, 1982); J. W. Wenham, *Easter Enigma* (Paternoster, 1984); N. T. Wright, *The Resurrection and the Son of God* (SPCK, 2017).

22 Acts 4:2.

23 1 Corinthians 15:6.

24 Jack C. Winslow, *Confession and Absolution* (Hodder & Stoughton, 1960), p. 22.

25 Matthew 26:28.

26 Romans 6:23.

27 1 Corinthians 15:14, 17–18.

28 Ephesians 1:18–20.

29 Bertrand Russell, *A Free Man's Worship* (1902; Unwin Paperbacks, 1976), pp. 10–17.

30 Graham McCann, *Woody Allen: New Yorker* (Polity Press, 1990), pp. 43 and 83.

31 Quoted in Frank Rich, 'Woody Allen Wipes the Smile off His Face', *Esquire*, May 1977, p. 75.

32 E.g. Philippians 3:21.

33 1 Corinthians 15:42–44.

34 1 Corinthians 15:20, 23.

35 Romans 8:29; Colossians 1:18; Revelation 1:5.

36 1 Corinthians 15:49.

37 Matthew 19:28.

38 Revelation 21:5.

39 Romans 8:20–23.

40 2 Peter 3:13; Revelation 21:1.

41 1 Peter 1:3.

42 Professor Oliver O'Donovan goes much further than this in his formative book *Resurrection and Moral Order: An Outline for Evangelical Ethics* (IVP and Eerdmans, 1986). He argues that the resurrection of Jesus is the foundation on which Christian ethics rests, because it proclaims that the created world order has been vindicated and reaffirmed by God; indeed, it has been redeemed, renewed and transformed. 'From the resurrection we look not only back to the created order which is vindicated, but forwards to our eschatological participation in that order' (p. 22), not only 'back to what is reaffirmed there, the order of creation', but also 'forward to what is anticipated there, the kingdom of God' (p. 26).

5 Jesus Christ is Lord

1 Romans 14:9 (RSV).

2 Romans 10:9.

3 1 Corinthians 12:3.

4 John 20:15.

5 Matthew 27:62–63.

6 Acts 2:21, 38.

7 Romans 10:12–13.

8 E.g. 1 Thessalonians 1:1; 3:11; 2 Thessalonians 1:2, 12; 2:16.

9 Cf. Acts 2:33–39.

10 Matthew 11:29.

11 2 Corinthians 10:5.
12 Dietrich Bonhoeffer, *The Cost of Discipleship* (1937; ET SCM Press, 1948), p. 31.
13 Romans 10:4 (RSV).
14 Romans 6:14.
15 Romans 8:4.
16 2 Corinthians 3:3, 6.
17 Jeremiah 31:33.
18 Ezekiel 36:27.
19 John 14:21.
20 Philippians 2:7.
21 Mark 10:45.
22 Luke 22:27.
23 Colossians 3:23–24.
24 Colossians 2:15.
25 Ephesians 1:20–22.
26 Matthew 28:18.
27 Ephesians 6:11–18.
28 1 John 5:19.
29 David W. Gill, *The Opening of the Christian Mind* (IVP USA, 1989), p. 131.
30 Mark 12:17.
31 Acts 17:7.
32 Revelation 1:5.
33 *Epistles*, 10:96.
34 E.g. Exodus 1:15–17; Daniel 3 and 6; Acts 4:19; 5:29.
35 Romans 13:1–7.
36 Acts 5:29.
37 *Institutes*, IV.xx.32.
38 Walter Bauer, *A Greek-English Lexicon of the New Testament and Other Early Christian Literature*, 2nd edn, translated and adapted by W. F. Arndt and F. W. Gingrich (University of Chicago Press, 1979).

Conclusion: The now and the not yet

1 Mark 1:15, as he translates *ēngiken*.

2 Matthew 12:28, *ephthasen*.

3 E.g. Mark 1:14–15; Matthew 13:16–17.

4 Matthew 12:28–29; cf. Luke 10:17–18.

5 Luke 17:20–21.

6 E.g. Mark 10:15.

7 Matthew 6:10.

8 Matthew 6:33.

9 Mark 9:47; cf. Matthew 8:11.

10 Matthew 25:34.

11 E.g. Isaiah 2:2; Matthew 12:32; Mark 10:30.

12 Galatians 1:4.

13 Colossians 1:13; cf. Acts 26:18; 1 Peter 2:9.

14 Ephesians 2:6; Colossians 3:1.

15 E.g. Matthew 13:39; 28:20.

16 Romans 12:2; 13:11–14; 1 Thessalonians 5:4–8.

17 Romans 8:24; 5:9–10; 13:11.

18 Romans 8:15, 23.

19 John 5:24; 11:25–26; Romans 8:10–11.

20 Psalm 110:1; Ephesians 1:22; Hebrews 2:8.

21 Romans 8:24.

22 Philippians 3:20–21; 1 Thessalonians 1:9–10.

23 Romans 8:19.

24 Romans 8:22–23, 26; 2 Corinthians 5:2, 4.

25 Romans 8:23; 1 Corinthians 1:7.

26 Romans 8:25.

27 E.g. Isaiah 32:15; 44:3; Ezekiel 39:29; Joel 2:28; Mark 1:8; Hebrews 6:4–5.

28 Romans 8:23.

29 2 Corinthians 5:5; Ephesians 1:14.

30 Hebrews 6:4–5.

31 Psalm 119:105.

32 2 Corinthians 5:7.

33 Deuteronomy 34:10; cf. Numbers 12:8; Deuteronomy 3:24.

34 1 Corinthians 13:9–12.

35 Deuteronomy 29:29.

36 1 Thessalonians 4:7–8.

37 Galatians 5:16–26.

38 2 Corinthians 3:18.

39 Galatians 5:17.

40 1 John 1:8.

41 Philippians 3:12–14; 1:6.

42 E.g. Leviticus 19:2.

43 John 8:11 (RSV).

44 E.g. Romans 7:17, 20; 8:9, 11.

45 2 Corinthians 12:12 (RSV).

46 Revelation 11:15 (RSV).

47 Hebrews 6:5.

48 2 Corinthians 4:10–11.

49 Revelation 21:5.

50 Ephesians 5:27; cf. Revelation 21:2.

51 1 Timothy 6:12.

52 Ephesians 4:3.

53 Matthew 13:30.

54 2 Peter 3:13; Revelation 21:1.

55 Mark 13:7.

56 Isaiah 2:4.

Enjoyed this book? Read the rest of the series.

With the God's Word for Today series, John Stott's classic book *The Contemporary Christian* is now available in five individual parts for today's audiences. The text has been sensitively modernized and updated by Tim Chester but retains the original core, clear and crucial Bible teaching.

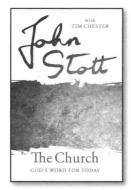

Find all five volumes at ivpress.com/god-s-word-for-today.

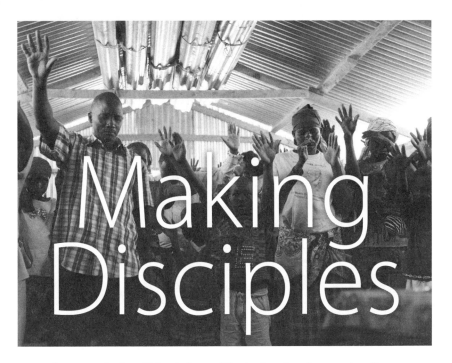

Making Disciples

Around the World — Christianity is exploding with growth in numbers

Yet — Believers are struggling to grow in Christ

That's Why Langham Exists

Our Vision

To see churches in the Majority World equipped for mission and growing to maturity in Christ through the ministry of pastors and leaders who believe, teach and live by the Word of God.

www.langham.org

FOUNDED BY JOHN STOTT

Langham®
PARTNERSHIP